INNOVATIVE
TECHNOLOGIES

BIOMASS ENERGY

ABDO
Publishing Company

INNOVATIVE TECHNOLOGIES

BIOMASS ENERGY

BY CAROL HAND

CONTENT CONSULTANT

Alaina L. Berger

Research Fellow, Department of Forest Resources

University of Minnesota

CREDITS

Published by ABDO Publishing Company, PO Box 398166, Minneapolis, MN 55439. Copyright © 2013 by Abdo Consulting Group, Inc. International copyrights reserved in all countries. No part of this book may be reproduced in any form without written permission from the publisher. The Essential Library™ is a trademark and logo of ABDO Publishing Company.

Printed in the United States of America,
North Mankato, Minnesota

092012
012013

 THIS BOOK CONTAINS AT LEAST 10% RECYCLED MATERIALS.

Editor: Melissa York
Series Designer: Craig Hinton

Photo Credits: Shutterstock Images, cover, 24, 29, 52, 74, 77, 83; Lijuan Guo/Fotolia, 6; Leonid Andronov/Shutterstock Images, 9; Red Line Editorial, 13, 47, 57; Stanislaw Tokarski/Shutterstock Images, 14; Fotolia, 17; Dee Marvin/AP Images, 21; Ted S. Warren/AP Images, 23; Rogello V. Solis/AP Images, 32; Paul Faith/AP Images, 34; Yuriy Kulyk/Shutterstock Images, 40; Boris Mrdja/Shutterstock Images, 43; Rolf Tumert/iStockphoto, 44; Andy Wong/AP Images, 51; Jean Schweitzer/iStockphoto, 54; Ed Kosky Jr./Allentown Morning Call/AP Images, 63; Carolina K. Smith/Shutterstock Images, 64; David J. Phillip/AP Images, 70, 97; Firma V/Shutterstock Images, 79; AZP Worldwide/Fotolia, 86; Dorling Kindersley/DK Images, 89; HJSchneider/Shutterstock Images, 91; Duluth News Tribune/AP Images, 94; Berca/iStockphoto, 101

Library of Congress Cataloging-in-Publication Data
Hand, Carol, 1945-
 Biomass energy / Carol Hand.
    p. cm. -- (Innovative technologies)
 Audience: 11-18.
 Includes bibliographical references.
 ISBN 978-1-61783-462-2
 1. Biomass energy--Juvenile literature. I. Title.
 TP339.H348 2013
 333.95'39--dc23
                    2012024005

≫ TABLE OF CONTENTS

CHAPTER 1

WHAT IS BIOMASS ENERGY?

Biomass is the oldest human energy source on the planet. Biomass energy in the form of heat is created every time organic matter is burned. People have burned wood for heat since they first discovered fire. As energy technologies continue to be developed, this ancient energy source is receiving more and more attention. In recent years, various sources of alternative energy—including biomass—have been taking hold in the United States and around the world. In 2006, *Nature* magazine stated, "Energy from biomass is an idea whose time has returned."[1] So what exactly is biomass energy, and why is it suddenly becoming popular again?

WHAT IS BIOMASS?

Matter can be either inorganic (nonliving) or organic (living). Biomass consists of any organic material, living or recently dead, that was originally produced by

« **Bonfires have been used for hundreds of years as a simple way to stay warm, as the burning wood releases heat.**

photosynthesis. During photosynthesis, energy from sunlight is stored in the roots, stems, and leaves of plants. Some of this energy is used by the plants, and some is transferred through the food web to animals, which ultimately depend on plants for food and survival. When plants and animals die, fungi and microorganisms break them down. Therefore, these organisms also depend on photosynthetic energy. This means all living material, from the smallest microbe to the largest tree, is biomass.

Biomass contains several types of organic chemicals, including carbohydrates, lipids, and proteins. These organic chemicals are extremely large molecules made of long chains of carbon atoms strung together. Elements such as hydrogen, oxygen, and nitrogen are also attached to these chains. The primary organic molecules burned for biomass energy are carbohydrates, which include starches and sugars, and lipids, which include fats and oils.

People burn various kinds of biomass to release its energy for heating homes, powering factories, and producing electricity. This combustion produces biomass energy, or bioenergy. Biomass can also be processed to produce transportation fuels similar to oil and gasoline. Plant material, particularly wood, is the most common source of biomass. But other biomass sources—for example, animal manure or industrial waste—can be used to provide heat, fuel, or power as well.

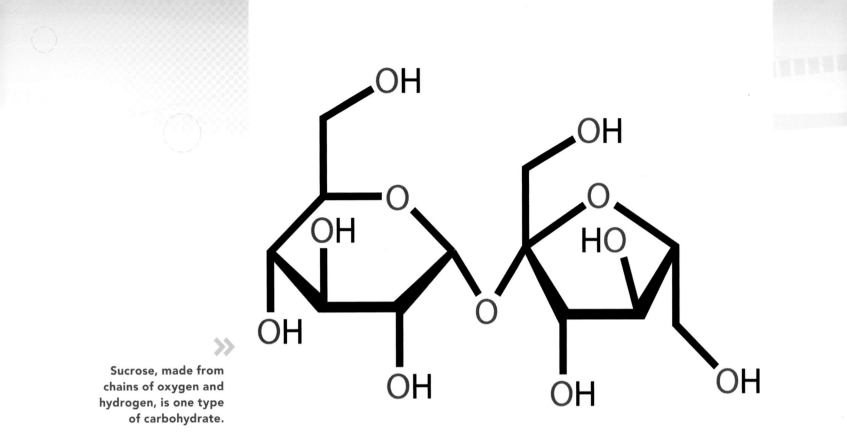

Fossil fuels include coal, oil, and natural gas. They are hydrocarbons, or molecules consisting of hydrogen and carbon. Most fossil fuels also contain some impurities. Similar to biomass, fossil fuels were formed from living organisms. But the organisms that made up fossil fuels lived long ago. After ancient organisms died, their remains became buried over time, and heat and pressure within the earth formed the fuels over millions of years.

THE LANGUAGE OF BIOMASS

Several similar terms are used to describe aspects of the field of biomass energy. Here are some important "biowords" to know:

» **Bioenergy:** biomass energy, or energy derived from biomass; usually describes electricity or heat produced from biomass
» **Biofuels:** one type of bioenergy; describes liquid fuels used for transportation, such as ethanol and biodiesel
» **Biogas:** a mixture of methane, carbon dioxide, and small amounts of other gases
» **Biopower:** biomass power, or the generation of electricity from biomass sources

WHY IS BIOMASS IMPORTANT?

Earth has a limited supply of fossil fuels. Humans are using fossil fuels at increasingly rapid rates, which will lead to their eventual depletion. As of 2012, fossil fuels supplied 85 percent of US energy needs.[2] As of 2011, the United States imported 45 percent of its oil from foreign sources.[3] The country uses military power to protect these sources. In addition, fossil fuel use contributes to many of the environmental problems currently facing the world. Fossil fuel use increases the concentration of greenhouse gases (GHGs) in the atmosphere. Most experts agree this intensifies climate change. Burning fossil fuels also causes pollution, including smog, oil spills, acid rain, and acid runoff from mines.

Biomass is one of several alternative energy sources that can help ease our dependence on fossil fuels. It is renewable, and with proper care, it can also be sustainable. That is, it can meet current and future energy needs without harming the environment, depleting the resource, or decreasing the land's ability to produce it. Biomass crops can be grown worldwide, unlike fossil fuels, which are only found in certain locations. The many potential biomass sources make biomass energy a particularly attractive fuel alternative. These sources include food crops, algae, trees and grasses, waste from cities and factories, and methane from landfills.

Biomass is not a silver bullet for solving the world's energy problems, but it can meet many local and regional energy needs. According to some biochemists, biomass can produce clean, abundant fuel for a large part of our expanding transportation system. The key is choosing beneficial, sustainable biomass sources while avoiding those that are likely to destroy ecosystems or pollute the atmosphere. At first glance, biomass may seem unimpressive—just a pile of garbage, a truckload of sawdust, or a field of grass. But with the right technology, this modest beginning can generate exciting ways to meet energy needs—from natural gas made from wood to algae-powered cars.

GREENHOUSE GASES AND CLIMATE CHANGE

Earth remains warm—averaging approximately 59 degrees Fahrenheit (15°C)—and able to sustain life because of tiny concentrations of GHGs that trap heat within the atmosphere. Important GHGs include carbon dioxide, methane, and nitrous oxide. They remain in the atmosphere for a long time. While GHG levels remain balanced, average temperatures do not change. However, people in modern times release large amounts of GHGs through fossil-fuel burning and land-use changes, including deforestation. This is increasing GHG concentrations in the atmosphere. Scientists find these increasing concentrations are causing a rise in global temperatures and associated climate changes. GHG increases are a major reason behind the push to develop alternatives to burning fossil fuels.

THE CARBON CYCLE

The total amount of carbon on Earth stays the same, but it cycles around Earth in different forms. Most carbon stays in the same place for periods of 100 to 200 million years. The largest carbon-storage areas are rocks, fossil fuels, and deep-ocean water and sediments. Natural processes such as rain, rock weathering, and volcanic explosions release bits of carbon from these reservoirs all the time. This is the slow carbon cycle.

Photosynthesis by land plants and aquatic microorganisms powers a seasonal cycle of carbon movement around Earth, known as the fast carbon cycle. Every spring and summer, these organisms absorb carbon dioxide from the air and water as they photosynthesize. Throughout the year, as all living organisms respire or die and decompose, they return carbon dioxide to the environment. Humans add stored carbon dioxide to the fast carbon cycle by the burning of fossil fuels and by deforestation.

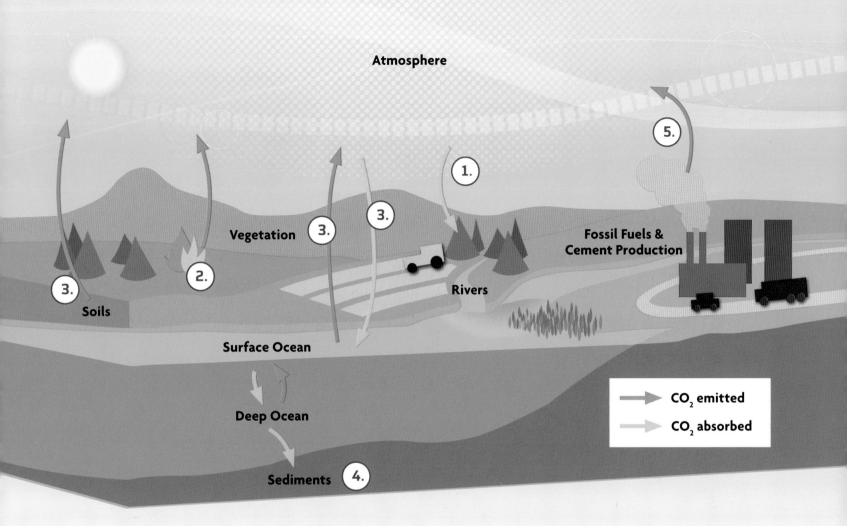

1. Plants absorb carbon dioxide in order to live.
2. When plants are burned, they release carbon into the air. When they decompose, their carbon goes into the soil.
3. Carbon also transfers between soil and air and between water and air.
4. The deep ocean and sediments below the ocean store large amounts of carbon.
5. The production of fossil fuels and products such as cement releases carbon that was stored in the soil millions of years ago.

CHAPTER 2

BIOMASS FROM PAST TO PRESENT

Evidence of early human ancestors using fire dates back at least 400,000 years. The control of fire made possible an explosion of new human activities, from cooking food to making weapons to driving animals from cover. The earliest fuels were natural, untreated biomass in the form of wood, peat, or animal dung. These fuels have low energy density because they are made up of a lot of water and other substances that do not produce energy. Because of their low energy density, it is inefficient to burn these fuels for energy.

USING UNTREATED BIOMASS

Historically, wood was the primary fuel source. Until the Industrial Revolution, wood met almost 91 percent of human energy requirements.[1] Through approximately 1910, wood was the major fuel used in rural US homes, and it is still the primary heating fuel

Masai men in Kenya demonstrate making a fire in the traditional way using brush and sticks.

in developing countries. Animal dung and plant debris, such as crop residues, remain important in regions with little or no industry, including parts of India and Africa. Into the 1990s, traditional fuels, including wood, charcoal, and nonwoody biomass, accounted for 60 percent of total energy use in sub-Saharan Africa, and up to 90 percent in some countries.[2] This has led to severe overcutting of trees in some areas.

THE INDUSTRIAL REVOLUTION

Coal mining—the first fossil fuel use—began in the thirteenth century when coal was used for forging and smelting metals. However, its use was not widespread until the Industrial Revolution, which began in Europe, particularly in Great Britain. A key new technology was steam power, developed in the seventeenth century by British inventors Thomas Savery and Thomas Newcomen and greatly improved in the eighteenth century by James Watt. By the seventeenth century, Britain began to experience wood shortages, and coal began to replace wood and charcoal for domestic uses. However, through approximately 1860 in the United States, wood was still the major fuel burned to produce steam for running industries, trains, and boats.

Because fossil fuels were concentrated and abundant, they gradually overtook biomass and dominated the energy field from the late nineteenth century through the twentieth century. After 1859, petroleum was becoming a popular energy source in the United States. Petroleum

As steam power grew more popular in the nineteenth century, coal began to replace wood and other biomass as an energy source.

was abundant and easy to drill and transport. By the early twentieth century, petroleum had overtaken both coal and biomass as the fuel of industry and transportation. Not only could petroleum be refined to make gasoline, kerosene, and other liquid fuels, but it was also the basis of many important consumer products, such as plastics.

BIOFUEL UPS AND DOWNS

Although fossil fuels eclipsed biomass as an energy source, two biofuels—ethanol and biodiesel—enjoyed intermittent surges in popularity. Their ups and downs followed world wars, price fluctuations, and political trends, but mostly they followed the fortunes of oil.

Ethanol is a type of alcohol made from plants. It can be used in place of gasoline in some motors. In the early nineteenth century, ethanol was important as a component of lamp fuel, and it was even consumed as a beverage. But beginning in 1862, it was taxed heavily to help pay for the Civil War. The tax made ethanol too expensive to use as a lamp fuel, and it was quickly replaced by petroleum-based oil. However, two transportation pioneers were convinced ethanol was the fuel of the future. In 1860, German engineer Nikolaus Otto, inventor of the modern internal combustion engine, used ethanol as the fuel in one of his engines. In 1896, US inventor Henry Ford designed his first car to run on ethanol. His 1908 Model T could run on ethanol, gasoline, or a combination—similar to today's flex-fuel cars. But even when the ethanol tax was repealed in 1906, gasoline remained less expensive, and ethanol did not replace it as the major transportation fuel.

Throughout the twentieth century, the popularity of ethanol continued to seesaw.

CHEMURGY AND FUEL ALCOHOL

In the 1930s, chemist William J. Hale and others began the chemurgy movement to promote the development of an agricultural fuel industry. In 1937, chemurgy proponents opened the Atchison Agrol Company in Atchison, Kansas. The company produced and sold Agrol, a blend of 10 percent fuel ethanol and gasoline. By early 1938, more than 2,000 gas stations offered Agrol.[3] But very low gasoline prices and strong opposition from petroleum supporters forced the company into bankruptcy by 1939.

Demand surged during World War I (1914–1918) but fell after the war due to low gasoline prices. The Twenty-First Amendment, which was in effect from 1920 to 1933, made it illegal to produce ethanol—a type of alcohol—as a beverage. Fuel alcohol was still legal, but it had to be mixed with petroleum to prevent people from drinking it. Even though fuel ethanol had advocates, the gasoline political lobby was stronger, and the ethanol industry was nearly shut down by 1939.

Demand for ethanol briefly surged again during World War II (1939–1945), but after the war, low petroleum prices encouraged fossil fuel use. Biomass-based fuel use died back once more. Then, in the 1970s, conflicts in the Middle East combined with increasing US dependence on Middle Eastern oil led to embargoes, shortages, and rapidly increasing oil prices. Rules restricting ethanol production were eased and production increased. Near the end of the twentieth century, another cycle of boom and bust occurred. In the 1980s, ethanol producers were going out of business, but after new government regulations in 1992 began encouraging the use of ethanol and gasoline blends, the business picked up once again.

Similar to ethanol, biodiesel has suffered throughout its history from competition with petroleum. The technology for producing biodiesel has changed little since the mid-nineteenth century. Rudolph Diesel, developer of the diesel engine, used peanut oil to fuel his first engine in 1898. Peanut, hemp, and corn oils were used as sources of biodiesel until the 1920s, when the diesel engine was modified so it could use petroleum diesel. Cheap oil, combined with the petroleum industry's powerful lobby speaking against the biomass industry, led to the steep decline of biodiesel.

Since the 1970s, biodiesel—like ethanol—has made a comeback. As of 2008, more than 700 fleets of US government vehicles ran on biodiesel, including fleets in the military, the US Post Office, national parks, and many school districts.[4] This number is increasing rapidly. Cities are also getting on the clean-fuel bandwagon, using biodiesel as well as other alternative fuel sources. By 2011, cities including Austin, Texas; Boulder, Colorado; and Knoxville, Tennessee, were using fleets that included biodiesel vehicles.

In the twenty-first century, biofuels seem poised to continue their latest surge in popularity. This time, oil prices seem unlikely to go down. Oil reserves are declining, and oil is becoming harder to obtain as its more accessible sources are used up. Meanwhile, world oil

WHAT IS BIODIESEL?

Biodiesel is made by distilling vegetable oils to produce two types of organic compounds: glycerin and esters. Glycerin is a major ingredient in soap. Esters are sweet-smelling substances often found in fragrances and flavorings. Methyl and ethyl esters result from distilling wood and grain oils, respectively. Either of these types of esters can be used as biodiesel fuel.

ATTENTION
IF PUMP RUNS
VERY SLOWLY
RELEASE
NOZZLE TRIGGER
COUNT TO 20 &
THEN TRY AGAIN

15

SOY
BIODIESEL™

» **Biodiesel is making a comeback as a popular substitute for traditional diesel.**

consumption continues to increase. As oil prices rise and shortages loom, we are also becoming aware of the dangers of climate change due to fossil fuel–based GHGs. Studies have now shown that use of 85 to 100 percent corn-ethanol fuel can decrease GHG emissions compared to regular gasoline.[5] Use of more sustainable biomass fuels and agricultural methods should improve fuel economy and decrease GHG emissions even further. Perhaps the time for biomass fuel has come at last.

In 1997, two young college graduates undertook a 10,000-mile (16,093-km) odyssey across the United States, trailing behind them the tantalizing smell of fresh french fries. The aroma came not from the travelers' lunches but from the tailpipe of their vehicle. Joshua and Kaia Tickell were traveling in the Veggie Van, a brightly painted 1986 Winnebago motor home with an unmodified diesel engine. The Veggie Van ran entirely on homemade biodiesel fuel created from used restaurant vegetable oil. The fuel burned 75 percent cleaner than petroleum-based diesel fuel.[6]

Before the tour, the Tickells carried out some very messy tests to get the diesel mixture just right. They did the tests in their Green Grease Machine, which they cobbled together from scrap parts. First, a juicer motor sucked used oil from a restaurant fryer, and then a converted tugboat fuel filter removed bits of french fries and other solids from the oil. The clean oil traveled into a converted military steam kettle, where an outboard boat motor stirred the diesel mixture, which included oil plus small amounts of methanol and lye. The Tickells tried various combinations of fryer grease and vegetable oil, and finally—covered in the oily stuff—they poured their best batch into their test vehicle, a diesel-engine Volkswagen. It worked!

The Veggie Van tour was designed to educate people about the possibilities of biodiesel fuel. The Tickells dreamed of "transforming the fast-food restaurant fryers of America into a

Inspired by innovators like the Tickells, more people are creating and using homemade biodiesel.

network of low-cost gas stations."[7] On the tour, they towed the Green Grease Machine behind the Veggie Van, producing biodiesel as they traveled. They visited many small towns, 20 major cities, and 25 states. Along the way, they gave presentations and appeared on national television shows. They talked to reporters, schools, and environmental organizations, answering thousands of questions about the Veggie Van. By the end of their tour, the Tickells were convinced that Americans wanted cleaner fuel and a cleaner society. They had proven that clean biodiesel fuel—biomass energy—could be produced with technology available to anyone.

CHAPTER 3

WHERE BIOMASS COMES FROM

Biomass exists almost everywhere. The two main types of biomass are wastes and crops. The biomass feedstocks for a region are often collected or grown locally. Thus, they vary from one place to another, depending on what is produced or thrown away in that area. Crop biomass is usually used to produce liquid biofuels, while forestry waste or municipal solid waste (MSW)—that is, garbage—is often burned to produce heat, electricity, or both.

Fossil fuels are high-density fuels; when burned, they release a large amount of energy compared to their volume. But unprocessed biomass has a relatively low energy density. For example, green wood consists of as much as 50 percent water.[1] Raw, unprocessed biomass is also inefficient to burn and expensive to transport long

« **Wood chips fly as loggers saw at a tree, leaving shavings that can later be used for energy.**

distances. The efficiency of raw biomass can be improved by processing it into liquid fuel or gases, or by drying, grinding, and pressing solid biomass into pellet form.

BIOMASS PELLETS: THE PERSONAL BIOMASS REVOLUTION

Although biomass has been used to cook food for millennia, recent innovations have the potential to revolutionize biomass use in the home. Pellet stoves using fuel pellets pressed from biomass such as sawdust, straw, corn stover, and sunflower hulls are increasing in popularity. Individuals either make their own pellets using miniature pellet mills or buy them ready-made. Dried, compressed biomass pellets have a much higher energy density than the raw feedstock. An Iowa company is popularizing the use of corn kernels (essentially nature-made pellets) to heat homes and small businesses. Stove owners simply dump measured amounts of corn kernels into their pellet stoves each day.

WASTE SOURCES OF BIOMASS

Waste biomass is potentially a large resource, and by using it to produce heat and energy, we decrease the problem of waste disposal. As of 2011, the largest sources of waste biomass were wood (including forestry waste of all kinds) and garbage (including MSW, manufacturing waste, and landfill gases). These sources are often used locally or regionally to provide energy for the industry that produced them or for nearby residents.

Forestry waste includes materials left after logging and materials produced during the manufacture of wood products. The largest sources of forestry waste, used to produce heat and electricity, are bark and sawdust left after milling wood and making paper. Other sources include shavings from production of wood products and "black liquor," a sludge-like liquid released from pulp and paper mills. In addition, much wood remains in the forest after logging. This includes dead and damaged trees, trees that are too small to log, and smaller branches and treetops. Some of these materials can be collected for biomass energy. However, removing too much material can destroy animal habitat and increase erosion. It also results in the loss of the nutrients that would be returned to the forest soil during decomposition of forest waste. Southeastern US forests require continuous fertilization because of poor soils, due in part to the removal of wood waste and understory growth during harvesting.

USING REGIONAL BIOMASS

The Oregon wood products industries illustrate the use of regional wood waste. According to the Oregon Department of Energy:

> Wood products industries burn wood chips, bark, and wood waste to supply heat for industrial processes. Some mills use biomass fuel to generate electricity for on-site uses. Pulp mills burn the residual fiber and lignin components of spent pulping liquor to recover and recycle pulping chemicals and to generate steam. Pellets and fuel logs manufactured in Oregon and firewood collected from Oregon forests supply heat to homes.[2]

MSW includes trash and garbage from homes, construction waste, and yard trimmings. When the organic portion of MSW decomposes in landfills, it produces methane gas. This gas can be captured to produce heat and power, thus preventing it from entering the atmosphere as a GHG. Solid material that is not placed in landfills may be burned to produce electricity. The United States currently has 87 waste-to-energy (WTE) plants, and approximately a dozen more plants or plant expansions are proposed.[3] WTE plants became less popular during the 1990s due to concerns about toxic emissions and likely contributions to GHGs. But with rising energy needs and landfill costs, these plants are making a comeback. Sanitation engineers stress that new smokestack scrubbers now prevent the release of toxic gases.

Agricultural waste can be either wet or dry. Dry wastes include poultry litter, animal bedding, feathers, straw, and corn stover (the leaves, husks, and stalks of corn that remain after the usable kernels have been removed). Wet wastes, including manure and grass, are inefficient energy sources because of their high water content. They must be dried before they are burned for energy.

FOOD AND ENERGY CROPS

Although wastes are important, crops are the major source of biomass energy, particularly for biofuels production. Biofuels are made from food crops, which may be used for either food

Corn and other crops are popular for making ethanol, competing with their use as a food source.

or energy. In the United States, the major food crops used to produce biofuels—also known as first-generation crops—are corn for ethanol production and soybeans for biodiesel. Food crops are very energy intensive, requiring fertilizers, pesticides, and energy for planting and cultivation. When used for biofuels, these crops also compete with food production, leading to increased food prices and loss of agricultural and forest land.

The future of biomass will depend on energy crops, or crops grown only to produce energy. These are also known as second-generation crops. Crops holding the most promise include

ETHANOL FEEDSTOCKS

First-generation food crops currently used to produce ethanol include:

> barley
> cassava
> corn
> sorghum
> soybeans
> sugar beets
> sugarcane
> wheat

Second-generation energy crops that will be used in the future include:

> bluegrass
> elephant grass
> fast-growing trees such as willow and poplar
> gamagrass
> switchgrass

native perennial grasses and short-rotation, or fast-growing, trees. The top perennial-grass candidate is switchgrass. Alfalfa, used for animal food, also shows potential because this highly productive perennial requires less fertilizer than many other crops. Short-rotation trees such as poplar, willow, sycamore, sweet gum, and cottonwood can reach heights of 40 feet (12 m) in eight years or less and can be harvested for up to 20 years before replanting. Harvesting is done by the process of coppicing, in which the trees are cut off at ground level and sprout again from the cut stump. Coppicing makes year-round harvesting possible and causes less environmental damage because trees are not replanted every year. Although short-rotation forestry has potential, it cannot currently produce enough biomass to meet the demand.

Researchers hope advances in genetics will allow them to produce varieties that grow faster and are adapted to a wider range of environments.

THREE ROUTES TO BIOFUELS

Developing biofuels that can replace today's fossil fuels is a priority in future biomass technology. These products must perform at least as well as the fuel they replace and must be both sustainable and affordable. As of 2012, three feasible technology pathways were being considered—oilseed, sugar, and lignocellulose/algae pathways.

The oilseed pathway is the short-term solution. It would extract oil from crops such as rapeseed (canola), jatropha, and camelina (false flax) to produce diesel, jet, and boiler fuel. Technology for this route is already well

BIODIESEL FEEDSTOCKS

Oil from almost any plant source can be used as a feedstock for making biodiesel fuel. The following crops are listed in decreasing order based on fuel yield:

- oil palm
- coconut
- jatropha
- rapeseed (canola)
- camelina (false flax)
- peanut
- sunflower
- safflower
- mustard
- soybean
- hemp
- corn

Other promising biodiesel feedstocks include used cooking oil, animal fat, and pond algae.

developed. The sugar pathway would also produce diesel, jet, and boiler fuel, and it would be an approach for the near and medium-term future. It depends on the sugarcane industry, which is already well established. Brazil is already using the sugar pathway, but the United States would need to scale up its technology of converting sugar to ethanol and develop technology for producing other biofuels from sugar for it to be a viable option.

The third pathway, converting lignocellulose and algae to biofuels, is a long-term solution. The molecules lignin and cellulose form the structural material of all plants. This material is usually discarded during harvest—for example, forestry waste and sugarcane stalks are full of both lignin and cellulose. Energy crops could also be grown to produce this material. But lignin and cellulose are extremely tough and hard to break down, and better technologies are required for both feedstock production and processing. The use of algae farms for biofuels is also currently in the research stage, but it holds promise for the future. Algae has a high oil content and can be grown and harvested rapidly in a much smaller space than other energy crops. The technology still needs to be developed for large-scale production and processing.

« A science museum in London, England, included exhibits about using algae for biofuel production.

CHAPTER 4

PROS AND CONS OF BIOMASS

There are a huge variety of biomass sources and almost as many ways to process and use these fuel sources. Whether a certain type of biomass is beneficial depends on the circumstances—the type of biomass and the location and conditions under which it is used. What is beneficial in one situation may be harmful in another. Additionally, two biomass sources may be beneficial compared to fossil fuels in a given situation, but one may be more efficient or sustainable than the other.

What are the required characteristics of a beneficial biomass source? The source must be readily renewable. It must be grown, collected, processed, and used cleanly and sustainably, minimizing environmental damage. It must not add carbon to the atmosphere. It must not take away land from food crops or forests. It must be abundant enough to provide a relatively high percentage of our energy needs for transportation,

« **Northern Ireland residents celebrate the installation of a new biomass fuel heating system that will reduce their carbon emissions.**

electric power, or heat. Finally, the technology for producing and using the biomass must be well developed and economically feasible.

The question is, how do we determine if a biomass source meets these criteria? One difficulty is that the source might have some positive characteristics, while other characteristics might make it unsustainable.

RENEWABILITY AND SUSTAINABILITY

Renewable energy sources are always available or can be replenished rapidly or continuously. Biomass from living crops can be rapidly regrown, and biomass from waste is constantly being produced. But being renewable does not always make a resource sustainable. Food crops require a lot of energy to grow, and if they are grown without sustainable farming techniques, they may cause harmful effects such as erosion or loss of soil nutrients.

Scientists stress the need to use biomass that can be sustainably produced. Sustainable production maintains both the biomass resource itself and the land's ability to produce more of it. Sustainable crops must be grown using methods that maintain water quality, soil productivity, wildlife habitat, and biodiversity. Carbon emitted into the atmosphere during production must be rapidly taken up by new plant growth, resulting in low overall carbon emissions. The biomass source should replace fossil fuel energy sources.

Trees and perennial grasses are more sustainable than annual crops because they are not replanted every year. They also protect the soil and the health and biodiversity of surrounding ecosystems much better than annual crops. Trees and grasses that are native to the region in which they are grown are the most sustainable. They are adapted to local conditions, so they require less energy input and disrupt the ecosystem less than food crops. They can often be grown on land that is too dry, hilly, rocky, or nutrient-poor to farm, so they do not compete with food crops. Their deep roots help them improve soil quality and prevent erosion. When used to make ethanol, grass and trees yield four to five times more energy than it takes

SUSTAINABLE PRODUCTION

Every resource, including biomass, undergoes a life cycle of production, use, and disposal. To determine the overall sustainability of the resource, scientists evaluate the energy and resources used as well as the environmental impacts resulting from all stages of the life cycle. The US Department of Energy's Biomass Program conducts studies that give some life-cycle information. Its studies determine the cost and availability of different types of biomass around the country. Studies also compare environmental effects related to production of each biomass type, including plant breeding, crop selection, and cultivation. Feedstock logistics studies cover efficient ways to harvest, store, and transport biomass feedstocks.

to grow them. When used in power plants to generate electricity, they may generate up to ten times more energy.[1]

Most experts agree that unless a biomass source can be produced and used sustainably, it should not be used to replace fossil fuels. If not grown and used sustainably, food crops, energy crops, and forestry and agricultural residues can cause environmental, social, and economic damage. To make biomass feedstocks more sustainable, farmers, foresters, and others in the field develop best management practices, or guidelines for growing and handling biomass. For example, farmers might leave some crop residues on the field to decrease erosion and help keep the soil fertile. Foresters might leave standing dead trees, large fallen trees, or trees with animal dens. These forest residues provide crucial animal habitat, protect soils from erosion, and replenish nutrients removed by harvesting. Both farmers and forest managers should plan harvesting to minimize soil disturbances. This includes using the correct type of machinery and timing harvests for when soil is less likely to compact or erode.

BIOMASS AND CLIMATE CHANGE

Under ideal circumstances, biomass is considered "carbon neutral." Living biomass is part of the present-day global carbon cycle. Its carbon has not been stored for millions of years, and therefore its release does not change the global carbon balance.

In the real world, though, the situation is not this simple. The farming, transportation, and manufacturing of biomass energy requires fossil fuel energy. Burning this energy adds GHGs to the atmosphere. The more fossil fuels a biomass source requires, the less carbon neutral and less sustainable it is. Also, changes in land use strongly affect carbon balance. Deforestation releases huge amounts of stored carbon from both trees and soil into the atmosphere. Up to 15 to 20 percent of worldwide carbon dioxide emissions result from deforestation and other land-use changes.[2] Sometimes, however, biomass production can improve carbon balance. For example, using damaged or marginal cropland to grow perennial biomass crops can increase carbon storage in plant roots and soil, decreasing its release into the atmosphere. Well-managed forests can also be carbon sinks, meaning they store more carbon than they release into the atmosphere. One proposed method for dealing with GHG emissions is to sell or trade carbon credits. That is, forests or other entities that store carbon can accumulate carbon credits, which can be sold or traded to organizations that release too much carbon into the atmosphere.

WHY IS BIOMASS CARBON NEUTRAL?

Biomass energy is part of the fast carbon cycle. During the biomass life cycle, photosynthesis removes carbon dioxide from the atmosphere, and an equal amount of carbon dioxide returns to the atmosphere when the biomass is burned as fuel. Thus, biomass can be a carbon-neutral fuel—it can be burned without causing a long-term net carbon dioxide increase. Fossil fuels, on the other hand, are part of the slow carbon cycle. Their carbon was removed from the biomass cycle millions of years ago and stored deep in the earth, away from the atmosphere. The burning of fossil fuels returns large amounts of this long-stored carbon to the atmosphere all at once, causing a rise in atmospheric carbon dioxide concentrations and unbalancing the world carbon cycle. For this reason, fossil fuels cannot be carbon neutral. They will always cause a net increase in atmospheric carbon dioxide.

If not managed properly, harvesting biomass can cause harmful effects such as deforestation.

BIOMASS AND POLLUTION

Pollution, particularly near-ground air pollution, is a serious concern when biomass—or any fuel—is burned. Air pollution varies with the type of biomass. The most pollution results from burning raw biomass, such as wood. This is one of several concerns raised by the environmental groups that opposed a large-scale biomass project in Vermont. They cited health effects caused by the ash and pollutants released by burning wood, including increased rates of asthma. The American Lung Association also opposes the use of wood biomass for energy because of its harmful health effects. The particles and toxic chemicals released by burning wood result in increased respiratory and heart disease, and some of the toxins released can cause cancer.

Burning MSW greatly reduces the amount of waste that must be disposed of in landfills, but it may also release harmful gases and toxins. In the United States, power plants that burn waste must follow strict guidelines for pollution control, including the use of technologies such as smokestack scrubbers, filters, and electrostatic precipitators, which are "static cling" devices that pull tiny particles out of air going up the smokestack. Disposing of the ash from these power plants is difficult if the original waste contained toxic metals such as lead or mercury. To prevent this problem, hazardous materials such as batteries and fluorescent lightbulbs

IS MSW RENEWABLE?

Not everyone considers MSW renewable. The Power Scorecard, sponsored by Pace University and several environmental groups, rated it as nonrenewable. MSW earned this rating because it includes materials made from fossil fuels and because its plant-based content, such as paper and wood, comes from sources that vary in sustainability. MSW power plants also release relatively high levels of GHGs and may cause pollution of the surrounding soil and water. In contrast, the US Environmental Protection Agency (EPA) and some state governments consider MSW renewable because it is abundant and contains large amounts of biomass. A power plant that follows the strict EPA guidelines should release minimum amounts of gases and toxic pollutants.

must be disposed of separately. Ash is tested; if safe, it can be used for other purposes, such as building roads.

BIOMASS AND THE LAND

Land-use changes have profound effects on ecosystems. Growing monoculture energy crops, particularly annuals, causes soil erosion and removes nutrients from the soil. Some farmers rely heavily on fertilizer or pesticides, leading to pollution and soil damage. In some cases, highly diverse ecosystems are destroyed to make way for energy crops. This is the case in Malaysia and Indonesia, where 25 million acres (10 million ha) of rich rain forests have been replaced with oil-palm plantations for biodiesel production.[3] In addition, water scarcity, loss of biodiversity, and increases in invasive species all tend to follow when land use moves from natural ecosystems to energy crops. Another serious problem is water supplies becoming overloaded with nutrients. Excess fertilizers washing off the cropland into water supplies cause explosions of algal growth. This in turn causes bacterial populations to grow, feeding on the algae as they die off. The bacteria use up oxygen in the water, causing fish and other aquatic animals to suffocate.

If biomass production is done correctly, it should reduce carbon emissions by decreasing fossil fuel use. It should provide employment for biomass producers, and it should reduce waste

Fertilizer runoff from farm fields can cause too much algae to grow in lakes and ponds.

from various sources. To produce energy, the best choice might be to plant a fast-growing, nonwoody crop such as switchgrass, which is both sustainable and rapidly replaced.

The risks of biomass production must be recognized and understood before they can be overcome, however. If we can overcome the risks, we can develop large-scale biomass production that is suited to the needs and environment of each region. The development of new energy crops and the tweaking of technologies to enable efficient production of second-generation fuels should make biomass more productive and more sustainable.

CHAPTER 5

BIOMASS ON THE RISE

Now, in the early twenty-first century, biomass energy is once more coming into its own. Due to climbing oil prices, dwindling reserves, and a warming climate, many countries are recognizing the benefits of all types of renewable energy. Indeed, many countries are setting targets for reducing nonrenewable energy use. Increased use of renewable energy sources, including biomass, is part of that equation. Biomass is plentiful and its technology is often simple, so it is again becoming a key renewable energy resource worldwide. In fact, biomass is the world's fourth-largest energy source after coal, oil, and natural gas.[1]

Direct burning of biomass continues to be the most common energy source in the developing world. Globally, 14 percent of primary (unprocessed) energy comes from biomass, usually wood or agricultural waste. In developing countries, these

« **Wood pellets are one of the many forms of biomass energy that are becoming more popular.**

sources supply an average of 38 percent of primary energy and as much as 90 percent in some countries.[2] Direct burning of biomass will likely remain important to developing countries for decades to come. Meanwhile, the developed world is beginning to return to biomass as a viable alternative energy source. However, it makes up a much smaller percentage of total energy than in the developing world. For example, in the United States, 4 percent of energy comes from biomass.[3] In Sweden, that number might reach as high as 32 percent.[4] Most of this biomass is used to produce electricity or is processed to make transportation fuels, particularly ethanol and biodiesel.

US BIOMASS ENERGY

According to the US Energy Information Administration, renewable energy of all kinds formed the smallest slice of the US energy pie in 2011 at only 9 percent. This 9 percent was further subdivided into seven kinds of renewable energy. Almost half of it came from biomass, including wood, biofuels, and biomass waste. A large percentage came from hydropower, with much smaller percentages from wind, solar, and geothermal energy.[5]

Until recently, the major forms of renewable energy in the United States were wood and hydroelectric power. Wood use has been relatively stable since 1949 and has contributed less to

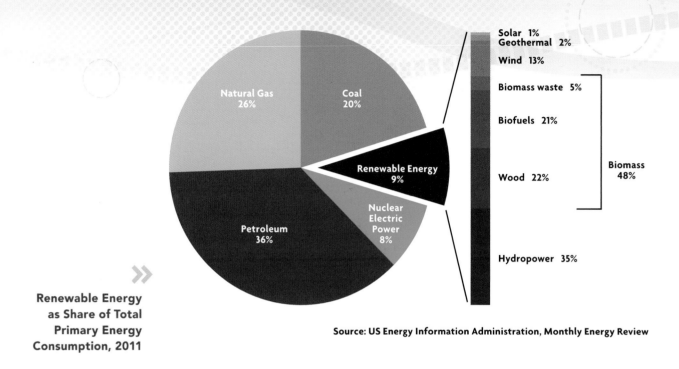

Solar 1%
Geothermal 2%

Wind 13%

Biomass waste 5%

Biofuels 21%

Natural Gas 26%

Coal 20%

Renewable Energy 9%

Biomass 48%

Wood 22%

Nuclear Electric Power 8%

Petroleum 36%

Hydropower 35%

Renewable Energy as Share of Total Primary Energy Consumption, 2011

Source: US Energy Information Administration, Monthly Energy Review

US energy than hydroelectric power. But beginning in approximately 1985, two other sources of renewable energy—wind and biofuels—took off and continue rising in importance.

US biomass production received a boost with the passage of the Energy Independence and Security Act (EISA) of 2007. This legislation requires improvements in vehicle gas mileage and the production of increased amounts of biofuels for transportation: 2 billion gallons (7.5 billion L) by 2012, and 22 billion gallons (83 billion L) by 2020. It further requires that biofuels achieve a 50 percent reduction in GHG emissions over the life cycle of the fuel, from production to use.[6]

BIOMASS ENERGY IN EUROPE

In the first decades of the twenty-first century, the member states of the European Union (EU) were trying to transition from fossil fuels to renewable energy resources. Approximately 70 percent of the renewables used in 2011 came from biomass sources. EU states have set individual goals for renewable energy use by 2020, increasing the percentage of their overall energy use that comes from renewable sources. These goals range from 49 percent for Sweden to 10 percent for Malta. The European Renewable Energy Council has set a further goal of using 45 percent renewable energy sources by 2030.[7]

Although the EU has made a start, it has a long way to go. In 2008, EU countries obtained 10.3 percent of their total energy from renewable sources, up from 8.9 percent in 2006. Use of biomass energy in the EU is expected to more than double by 2020, mostly due to increased use of energy crops, agricultural by-products, and wood residues from logging.[8]

THE KYOTO PROTOCOL

In 1997, more than 190 nations ratified the Kyoto Protocol. Its goal was to slow climate change by requiring each nation to set goals for decreasing GHG emissions. The United States refused to ratify the agreement, saying it "wrongly omitted developing nations."[9] Many member nations in the developed world are trying to meet their Kyoto goals—with mixed success—by using renewable energy sources. In December 2011 in Durban, South Africa, a new global agreement was made. It established a multibillion-dollar fund to aid developing nations in responding to climate change and also extended the Kyoto Protocol in Europe for another five years. The results of this successor to the Kyoto Protocol were inconclusive, however, as participants ended the conference with a new deadline to write a new agreement by 2015.

Workers at a Chinese wheat farm shovel waste into a prototype biomass machine that will produce pellets for use at a nearby factory.

BIOMASS ENERGY IN CHINA

China, with its huge population and rapidly developing economy, is also taking biomass energy seriously. Chinese industry has remained very dependent on coal, which causes significant pollution and GHG emissions. In 2006, China passed the United States as the world's largest emitter of carbon dioxide.[10] But China's renewable-energy industry is also growing rapidly.

In 2006, its production of wind turbines and solar cells more than doubled.[11] Biomass energy is expected to grow rapidly in the coming years. Presentations at a 2011 Biomass Energy Exposition in Beijing emphasized China's determination to develop biomass energy. They plan to use waste straw, currently burned in the fields, as a fuel for power plants. They also plan to produce biomass pellets from forestry waste, straw, and urban greenery for use in boilers instead of coal or oil. These uses of biomass would reduce both solid waste and GHG emissions.

Biofuels, both ethanol and biodiesel, are also part of China's biomass energy tool kit. As of 2012, China ranked third worldwide in total biofuel production after the United States and Brazil.[12] Most of China's ethanol is made from corn, but the country is in the process of replacing corn with other feedstocks. For example, in 2011, 98 percent of the cassava root exported from Thailand went to China for biofuel production.[13] Chinese producers are also using sweet potato and sorghum to make ethanol. Most of the small amount of biodiesel currently produced comes from waste vegetable oil. Various oilseed crops are being considered, but some potential oilseed crops compete with food crops. Other oilseed crops, such as palm oil, are imported and cause deforestation in their source countries. By 2020, China plans to produce 30 percent of its aviation fuel from other biomass sources, including algae and waste oil.[14] To meet its future biomass needs, China will have to balance many factors, including food, environmental, and economic needs.

Sugarcane is an important source for ethanol production in Brazil, which leads to competition with land used for food crops.

BIOFUELS ON THE RISE

One major use for petroleum is as fuel for cars, trucks, trains, and airplanes. Developing replacements for gasoline and diesel fuel is a high priority in the biomass industry, and the recent rise of ethanol and biodiesel around the world shows the success of this effort. Since 2000, world biofuel production has more than quadrupled, from 4.8 billion gallons (18 billion L) in 2000 to 21 billion gallons (79.5 billion L) in 2008. Still, this accounts for only approximately 1 percent of global fuel consumption for transportation.[15]

WHAT IS RAPESEED?

Rapeseed, also known as canola, is a member of the mustard family that has very high concentrations of oil and protein. For centuries, rapeseed has been used as both food and fuel oil. It is currently the source of canola oil used in cooking and the major feedstock for production of biodiesel in the EU.

By far the largest ethanol producers are the United States and Brazil, followed by the EU, China, and Canada. The main ethanol feedstock in the United States is corn, while Brazil uses sugarcane. World biodiesel production is small but growing rapidly, with the output increasing from 230 million gallons (870 million L) in 2000 to 3.9 billion gallons (14.8 billion L) in 2008. The EU leads in biodiesel production. It produces nearly 80 percent of the world's total, using rapeseed as its major feedstock. The United States is second, and Brazil is third.[16]

The upsurge in biofuel production has led to serious problems. World food, feed grain, and soybean prices have increased dramatically. There is strong competition for land to produce biofuels instead of food and forest crops. Production of biofuels is also causing environmental damage, and so far it has not decreased GHG emissions, at least in the United States. Thus, there is still much work remaining to improve biomass and biofuel technologies and to ensure they are efficient processes that help, rather than hurt, the world's energy situation.

CHAPTER 6

MAKING AND USING BIOPOWER

The simplest and oldest method of using biomass is burning it directly to produce heat—for example, in a home fireplace or stove. In this case, biomass is both the feedstock and the fuel—that is, it is not processed in any way before it is used. However, this raw biomass is an inefficient source of energy.

Biomass is processed on a much larger scale to generate biopower—electricity that can power industries or whole cities. Generation of electric power always follows the same basic process, regardless of the original fuel source. First, a fuel is burned at high temperatures, producing steam. The steam runs a turbine that is connected to a generator. The generator transforms the mechanical energy of the spinning turbine into electric power. Most power plants burn coal, oil, or natural gas as the fuel. But now and in the future, biomass power plants in which all or part of the fuel is wood waste,

« **Researchers are developing more advanced technologies for renewable energy, such as this energy plant in Denmark.**

MSW, or some other biomass source will become more common. Technologies used to produce biopower include direct firing, cofiring, gasification, and anaerobic digestion.

DIRECT FIRING AND COFIRING

In direct firing, solid biomass is the fuel source burned to produce steam and ultimately generate electric power. Power plants that burn only biomass are often combined heat and power (CHP) plants, which produce both electricity and heat for heating buildings and running industrial processes. Most CHP plants are only approximately one-tenth as large as coal-fired plants: CHP plants produce from 1 to 100 megawatts of power, while the average size of a coal-fired plant is approximately 667 megawatts.[1] The smaller size of CHP plants is due to lower availability of local biomass fuel and higher costs of transporting it from elsewhere. CHP plants are often used to dispose of MSW and crop by-products such as wood chips and sugarcane waste. The percentage of fuel converted into usable electricity in a typical CHP plant is

KODA ENERGY

Koda Energy, a Minnesota CHP plant that opened in 2009, is the only CHP plant in the United States that burns entirely non-man-made biomass products. It burns regional agricultural by-products, including oat hulls from the General Mills cereal factory, sunflower hulls, and wood shavings. Koda Energy also burns by-products from Rahr Malting Company, which processes malt, a beer ingredient made from barley. The CHP plant's energy conversion efficiency is approximately 87 percent, compared to 63 percent for a coal-fired power plant.[2] Rahr Malting Company uses heat from the Koda Energy plant in its malting process. Both Koda and Rahr use the electricity produced, and excess power is sent to the regional power grid. Koda Energy meets Minnesota's green energy requirements. It also does research on converting marginal land to biomass production and using native prairie plants as fuel.

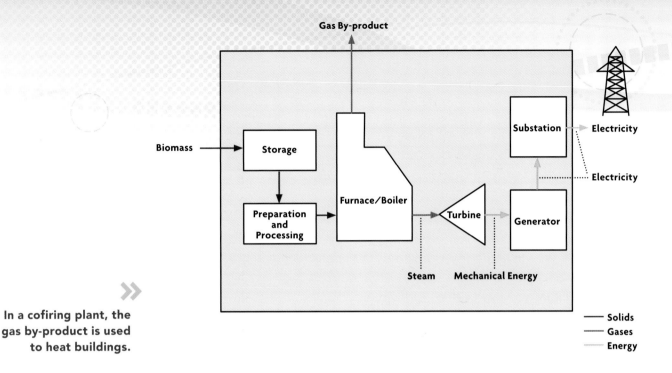

Gas By-product

Biomass → Storage

Preparation and Processing

Furnace/Boiler

Turbine

Steam   Mechanical Energy

Generator

Substation → Electricity

Electricity

In a cofiring plant, the gas by-product is used to heat buildings.

— Solids
— Gases
— Energy

approximately 30 to 34 percent, similar to a basic natural-gas power plant. However, factoring in the production of heat, a CHP plant's total efficiency can reach 85 to 90 percent.[3]

Cofiring is the combined burning of coal and biomass in power plants designed to burn only coal. Existing power plants usually need only minor changes to use cofiring. Adding biomass to the coal reduces toxic emissions, including sulfur and mercury, and can lower carbon emissions. By mixing coal with up to 10 percent biomass, overall power plant efficiencies can be increased. In fact, by using local, low-cost biomass, the necessary upgrades can be paid for in approximately two years due to the energy produced by increased efficiency. However, this is only possible with high-quality biomass such as dry wood biomass, crop residues, and crops—not wet wood or crops with high water content. Cofiring plants are operating successfully in the United States, Australia, and northern Europe. In some cases, coal-fired power plants can be refitted to run on biomass alone, a process known as repowering. Natural-gas plants can be converted to run on biogas rather than fossil fuel–based natural gas.

GASIFICATION

In gasification, small amounts of oxygen break down biomass feedstocks into simpler molecules without burning them. Industries have used gasification for more than 75 years to produce chemical products, and the electric power industry is now using this technology to produce gas for generating electricity.

The primary product of gasification is synthetic gas, or syngas, which is a mixture of carbon monoxide, carbon dioxide, and hydrogen gases. MSW is a typical feedstock. During gasification, the MSW is shredded into small particles. Next, a measured amount of air or oxygen is injected into the waste, and everything is heated to 1,100 to 1,800 degrees Fahrenheit (600 to 1,000°C). After the syngas is produced, impurities are removed. The purification process minimizes pollution.

An exciting new method of gasification is plasma gasification. Plasma is formed when an electric charge passes through a gas. A lightning flash is one example of plasma. Plasma gasification occurs at temperatures up to 10,000 degrees Fahrenheit (5,500°C)—much higher than normal gasification temperatures. These high temperatures speed up gasification reactions and keep them going. Any impurities present are melted and fused into materials that can be used for other purposes, such as road construction. Use of plasma gasification in the WTE industry is very new. Plants that use this technology have opened in Japan, Canada, and India, and several have been proposed in the United States.

INCINERATION VERSUS GASIFICATION

Gasification is different from incineration. In incineration, MSW is burned directly as a fuel, producing carbon dioxide, heat, and ash as waste products. This is much like burning a pile of trash in the backyard, except it is enclosed. The MSW is not cleaned before use, so its contaminants literally go up in smoke. This leads to the need for pollution control systems.

In gasification, when the MSW is used as a feedstock, it produces a fuel as a product. This fuel, syngas, burns much cleaner than the MSW and can be used to generate electricity or processed further into products with higher energy densities, such as hydrogen, ethanol, and substitute natural gas, a synthetic product that can be used in place of the fossil fuel.

ANAEROBIC DIGESTION

Bacterial production of gases without using oxygen is called anaerobic digestion. In this process, bacteria consume and break down moist and wet wastes, including manure, food processing wastes, and municipal sewage. Anaerobic digestion occurs naturally in landfills and produces biogas, also called landfill gas. Biogas is a mixture of 40 to 75 percent methane gas, plus small amounts of carbon dioxide, hydrogen sulfide, and ammonia.[4] Biogas is particularly important as a replacement for natural gas, which is also primarily methane. After it is collected, biogas can be further processed to separate out the methane, producing a fuel that is equal to or better in quality than natural gas. On farms, anaerobic digestion removes bacteria from manure, a major source of water pollution. The remaining solids, which contain high levels of nutrients, can be sold as fertilizer.

Anaerobic digestion is often used on farms and in small MSW plants, where the biogas is collected and burned to generate heat and power. It can also work in larger heating plants, replace natural gas, or function as a transportation fuel. Methane, the main component of biogas, is an efficient fuel source but is also a powerful GHG. However, collecting waste methane and burning it as a fuel prevents it from entering the atmosphere, so it does not contribute to global warming.

THE PROMISE OF BIOPOWER

In 2009, the United States obtained more than 50 billion kilowatt-hours of electricity—approximately 1.5 percent of its total electricity—from biomass sources.[5] While this is a significant amount, most of it is based on the use of wastes such as forestry waste and MSW, which are limited in supply and not always available.

Scientists expect that as biomass technology improves and more emphasis is placed on growing energy crops for power generation, the contribution of biopower could greatly increase. Several organizations have estimated the potential of biopower. These estimates vary greatly because organizations make different assumptions about resources available, harvesting

ANAEROBIC DIGESTION TECHNOLOGY

On farms, manure digestion using anaerobic digestion technology began in the 1970s. Airtight chambers, or digesters, range from simple covered lagoons to complex flow systems such as plug-flow digesters. In plug-flow digesters, the waste is continuously pushed through long chambers with separate regions for mixing and digesting. All digesters have impermeable covers under which biogas collects. Oregon's Tillamook Digester Facility, opened in 2003, uses an anaerobic digestion process for regional electricity production. The facility receives manure from dairy farms and processes it in two 400,000-gallon (1.5 million L) digester cells. Biogas is produced and used to run two Caterpillar engines, each attached to a 200-kilowatt generator. The generated electricity is sold to the Tillamook People's Utility District.

Anaerobic digestion is also used to treat MSW and wastewater. This decreases the amount of MSW going to landfills, stabilizes the organic material to prevent future air and water pollution, and recovers biogas. In wastewater treatment, it reduces the volume of sewage sludge and destroys bacteria. In Portland, Oregon, the Columbia Boulevard Wastewater Treatment Plant uses a fuel cell to convert biogas into electricity. The fuel cell has operated since 1999, producing an estimated 1.5 million kilowatt-hours of electricity per year.[6]

practices, and other factors. For example, in 2007, the Energy Information Administration estimated that by 2025, biomass could provide approximately 12 percent of US energy needs. However, the Union of Concerned Scientists' estimate was much lower, predicting biomass could provide only 7.2 percent of the country's energy needs.[7] This lower estimate took into account potential conflicts between food production and energy production and assumed biomass production and use would be completely sustainable.

A farmer uses a small anaerobic digester to turn pig manure into energy. ≫

CHAPTER 7

BIOFUELS: BIODIESEL

Heat and electricity are produced by converting biomass through combustion, gasification, and bacterial digestion, among other processes. Technology for these processes already exists and will likely continue to increase in efficiency. But most future emphasis in bioenergy will be on biofuels. The most common biofuels are ethanol and biodiesel. According to the International Energy Agency, global biofuel production will quadruple by the year 2027, providing 10 percent of the world's transportation fuel.[1]

MAKING BIODIESEL

Biodiesel fuel feedstocks are varied and widely available, and some produce very high oil concentrations. The production process is simple and can be done on either a very small scale, producing batches just large enough to supply a single car, or a very large

« The use of biofuels such as ethanol and biodiesel is predicted to increase dramatically in the near future.

scale, producing the fuel continuously in a large factory. Biodiesel is also clean-burning and nontoxic compared to petroleum diesel, although its energy content is somewhat lower. It is safe to transport and store, and it can be blended with petroleum diesel in any percentage.

For most of the twentieth century, diesel engines were adapted to run efficiently using petroleum-based diesel fuel. When biodiesel began to make a comeback late in the century, existing diesel engines could not use unprocessed vegetable oil as a fuel. Researchers decided it was easier to change the fuel than the engines.

Biodiesel production depends on oil crops. Europe produces more than 80 percent of the world's biodiesel. In 2006, biodiesel was used for 55 percent of the EU's transportation needs. US biodiesel production is increasing, and by 2006, the United States had passed every country except Germany.[2] Growth is still slowed by availability of feedstocks, but world biodiesel production is expected to rapidly increase in the future. Currently, most biodiesel is processed from food crops such as soy, rapeseed, and palm oil, but production is rapidly moving to the

THE CHEMISTRY OF BIODIESEL

Biodiesel is composed of esters. These simple organic compounds are made by mixing two smaller compounds: a fatty acid and an alcohol. Three ingredients are required to make biodiesel: the plant oil, an alcohol (usually ethanol or methanol), and small amounts of a catalyst (usually sodium hydroxide, commonly known as lye). Plant oils are triglycerides, which consist of three fatty acids linked to a single glycerin molecule. Glycerin makes the plant oil too thick to be a good fuel by itself. To get from plant oil to biodiesel, the first step is to separate the three fatty acids and remove the glycerin from the oil. This is the catalyst's job. It "cracks" the oil, or starts the chemical reaction between the triglyceride and the alcohol. After the fatty acids are separated, an alcohol molecule attaches to each fatty acid to make three esters (biodiesel molecules). The esters are much more watery than the original oil.

cheaper nonfood crops. One option is jatropha, now being planted on a large scale in China, India, Brazil, and several African countries. Castor beans are another potential biodiesel source, as well as food crops including sunflowers, soybeans, palm, peanuts, and cotton.

BIODIESEL FROM ALGAE

Even the cleanest, most sustainable sources of biomass require large tracts of land for production. In addition, they take a minimum of one year to produce a crop. What if, instead, we could produce large quantities of biomass in a limited space with a process that takes a few days instead of a year? As it happens, we can.

The biomass crop is single-celled algae, or microalgae. Pond scum is one example. This is not really such an unusual energy source—much of the world's petroleum began as algae in ancient, shallow oceans.

WHAT IS JATROPHA?

Jatropha curcas is a drought-resistant, nonedible tree or shrub. It lives up to 50 years and produces seeds with high oil content. It is found around the world in tropical and subtropical areas and will survive light frosts. It will grow almost anywhere, but it is particularly adapted to dry habitats and survives well in poor soils. *Jatropha curcas* has been used as a medicine for many years, but most recently, it has become the major feedstock for the production of biodiesel. Its seeds contain from 37 to 60 percent oil.

A US Department of Energy research project from 1976 to 1998 used carbon dioxide retrieved from coal-burning power plants to grow algae in ponds. One result of this project was identification of some 3,000 species of algae that can be used to produce biodiesel.[3] In theory, microalgae—considered a third-generation biofuel—could produce 100 times more oil per acre than soil-based biodiesel crops. Microalgae also do not compete with food crops, may be grown in wastewater, and are carbon neutral if the waste left after harvesting the algae is used to power the fuel-processing system.

Algae can be grown in many types of systems, including open or closed ponds, sewage or wastewater, and both freshwater and saltwater. The species grown varies with the system, and the systems vary in terms of cost, ease of handling, and yield of algae. For example, open ponds are relatively inexpensive and easy to construct, but controlling conditions such as weather changes or contamination is difficult, and water is lost to evaporation. Closed ponds have covers similar to greenhouses. They allow more control over environmental conditions, but they are more expensive, and the potential size of the operation is smaller.

Algae can also be grown in a photobioreactor (PBR)—a closed-flow system. In a PBR, algae are pumped through tubes including a feeding vessel and a built-in cleaning system. When sensors detect a level of oxygen indicating enough photosynthesis has occurred, it is time for harvest. PBRs are more expensive than ponds but give higher yields.

During harvest, the algae are separated from their growing environment. Water is removed until the remaining algae form a thick paste. The harvested algae are then processed to remove the oil. This is the most expensive part of the process, and research continues on how to do it efficiently. Extraction can be either mechanical or chemical. Mechanical methods include pressing the cells or breaking them apart with ultrasound. These methods are expensive and energy intensive because they usually require drying the algae. Chemical methods use solvents that may cause health and safety issues.

Fuel from algae is not a perfect solution. It is still expensive to produce: in 2009, it cost approximately eight dollars per gallon ($2.10/L) according to the US Department of Energy.[4] Costs can be lowered by using waste heat from the system and by selling by-products to

RUNNING ON ALGAE

Sapphire Energy, a California-based company, makes biofuel from algae. Sapphire Energy produces green crude, which has the same composition as petroleum-based crude oil and can therefore be used in existing oil refineries to produce a variety of oils and gases. Former Sapphire CEO Jason Pyle is convinced algae biodiesel production can be scaled up for commercial use. "I think algae is one of the only viable technologies for this," he said. "What else can scale to 10 billion, 50 billion gallons [38 billion, 189 billion L]? Very few sources."[5] Pyle points out that algae does not require arable land or drinkable water (he uses seawater), and therefore it can be grown rapidly and cheaply.

In 2009, the company unveiled the Algaeus, a hybrid car built into the shell of a Toyota Prius. The Algaeus can run on electricity and green crude instead of gasoline. Researchers are also experimenting with algae-fueled motorcycles.

Tim Zenki from Sapphire Energy presents beakers filled with algae and algae-based biodiesel, showing the process of making the fuel.

add to animal feed and for other purposes. Additionally, an important assessment of algae biofuel production, published in 2010, suggested current methods are not yet sustainable. The study found that algae production consumes more energy, releases more carbon dioxide into the atmosphere, and uses more water than other sources of biofuel, including switchgrass, rapeseed, and even corn. This is because the algae must be fertilized, and often the fertilizer used is petroleum based. Not all algae companies use petroleum-based inputs, but the study indicates that if they do, they are not producing sustainable fuels.

Exciting research into microalgae as a biofuel continues. The genetic codes of two marine microalgae species have recently been unraveled. This will make possible the bioengineering of new algal strains that produce more oil, grow faster, or have other characteristics that make them better fuel sources. Oak Ridge National Laboratory in Tennessee also has ongoing research projects to address several factors limiting development of algal fuel. Among other things, workers there are trying to come up with new technologies for decreasing the cost of carbon dioxide for algal growth, new and better PBR designs, and new techniques for harvesting and drying the algae.

USING BIODIESEL

As of 2008, in both the United States and Europe, nearly 70 percent of petroleum products were used for transportation. For automobiles, by far the most common fuel is gasoline. But for other vehicles—trucks, buses, trains, mass transit, boats, farm equipment, and airplanes—the most common fuel is diesel. Diesel-powered automobiles have shown only sporadic popularity in the United States, while their use continues to grow in Europe. Only approximately 3.5 percent of US passenger vehicles were diesel powered, and most of these were pickup trucks. In Europe, approximately 50 percent of cars were diesel powered.[7] All types of vehicles are potential users of biodiesel, either by itself or combined with petroleum diesel. In addition, smaller electric generators—for example, emergency generators for homes and hospitals—are potential biodiesel users. Biodiesel can also be used as an additive or replacement for heating fuel in oil-fired furnaces or boilers.

Biodiesel has many potential uses; however, unless production and sustainability problems with biodiesel crops can be overcome, its use may be limited. Many people thought as gasoline and conventional diesel prices rose, biodiesel would become more affordable, but this has not happened. Biodiesel prices are rising too, partly because the oil crops are also used for food

SOLIX BIOSYSTEMS

Solix's Lumian AGS4000 is an algal growth system consisting of floating panels that allow concentrated growth of algae outdoors. The algae are actually grown inside the panels rather than in open ponds. Solix's demonstration plant, located at Coyote Gulch in southwestern Colorado, opened in 2009 and is the first of its kind. Its three algae cultivation basins use wastewater generated during coal mining, thus decreasing the need for freshwater. Carbon dioxide captured from a nearby chemical plant is sent through the Lumian panels to feed the algae. The algae produced at Coyote Gulch are converted to oil and residual biomass. As of 2009, Solix BioSystems removed the oil using chemical solvents—a potential health and environmental hazard—but the company was developing technology that uses sound waves to blast the algae, making oil extraction easier, cheaper, and more environmentally friendly.

and partly because biofuel production uses petroleum-based chemicals. Since 2008, biofuel plants have been closing in many countries, including the United States and members of the EU. Some organizations are very optimistic about biofuels, however. One study predicted average increases in the global market of approximately 42 percent per year through 2016.[8] Almost everyone seems to agree on two things:

1. There are great opportunities for regional development of biofuels from waste oils and small-scale, local, and ecologically sustainable production of oil crops.

2. The price of biodiesel (compared to petroleum-based diesel) must decrease if it is to become a competitive fuel in the United States. This will require the development of new feedstocks with much higher oil concentrations than soybeans, which are currently the US staple for biodiesel. This in turn means second-generation crops must be developed, particularly algae.

CHAPTER 8

ETHANOL

Ethanol is one of many types of alcohol. All alcohol molecules have the same general formula but different numbers of carbon atoms. The two simplest alcohols are methanol and ethanol. Methanol, also called wood alcohol because it can be made from wood, is extremely toxic. Ethanol, besides being an excellent fuel, is the same alcohol found in alcoholic beverages including beer and wine.

MAKING ETHANOL

Ethanol is produced by fermentation, a process by which oxygen breaks down sugars and starches. Fermentation is a relatively simple chemical process, and people have used it to produce alcoholic beverages for at least 8,000 years. Sugarcane and sugar beets contain sugars ready to ferment. Starch crops such as corn must first be broken down into smaller, fermentable sugar molecules. Yeast is then added to ferment the

« The process of fermentation extracts ethanol by breaking down starches such as corn.

sugars. This produces a beer containing 10 to 12 percent ethanol. The beer is distilled to obtain 80 to 95 percent ethanol and then further dehydrated to produce 100 percent ethanol, which can be used as vehicle fuel.[1]

Many different biomass sources can be used to produce ethanol. First-generation sources are usually food crops—for example, corn in the United States and sugarcane in Brazil. Corn ethanol has many advantages. It is renewable, and corn is rapidly grown. It reduces US dependence on foreign oil. Compared to gasoline, it reduces toxic air pollutants and smog formation. When used as an additive, ethanol reduces engine knocking or pinging. It is relatively inexpensive to produce, and it supports rural economies and increases local and state tax revenues.

But corn ethanol also has disadvantages. Corn and other ethanol crops are usually not grown sustainably, and they use land that would otherwise be used for food production. Although excess GHGs are not released when corn ethanol is burned, they are released

TYPES OF ETHANOL

No car presently on the market burns pure ethanol in place of gasoline; instead, the two fuels are blended. The most common blend is E10, which is gasoline containing 10 percent ethanol. As of 2011, ethanol levels up to 10 percent were found in 95 percent of US cars.[2] These low levels increase power, help fuel burn cleaner, and prevent engine knocking without the health and pollution hazards of other gasoline additives. A second blend, E85 or flex fuel, can be used only in specially modified vehicles. It contains between 51 and 83 percent ethanol, depending on season and geography.[3] The gasoline content enables it to be used during cold weather, when pure ethanol burns poorly. E85 is now available in more than 40 states, but only at a limited number of gas stations. It is most common in the Corn Belt states, including Illinois, Indiana, Iowa, Michigan, Minnesota, Missouri, and Wisconsin.

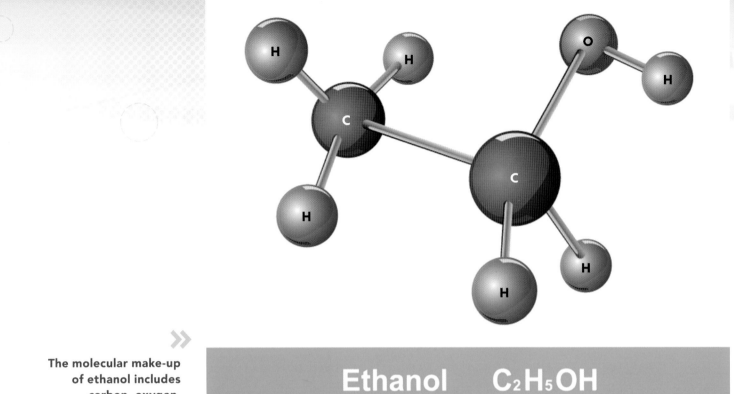

The molecular make-up
of ethanol includes
carbon, oxygen,
and hydrogen.

Ethanol   C₂H₅OH

during the corn's growth and processing. Corn growth and ethanol production both use a lot of energy. Ethanol can be more expensive to buy than gasoline, and it contains less energy than gasoline, meaning cars using ethanol get fewer miles per gallon. Ethanol is not a perfect alternative energy source, and its production and use are controversial. There are debates about the energy balance of ethanol, the food-versus-fuel question, and the land-use problem.

ENERGY BALANCE

Fossil fuel energy balance is the ratio of how much energy is needed to make ethanol versus how much energy it delivers when burned as fuel. James B. Meigs, the editor-in-chief of *Popular Mechanics*, points out:

> *Corn doesn't grow like a weed. Modern corn farming involves heavy inputs of nitrogen fertilizer (made with natural gas), applications of herbicides and other chemicals (made mostly from oil), heavy machinery (which runs on diesel), and transportation (diesel again). Converting the corn into fuel requires still more energy.*[4]

A negative energy balance means more energy is used to make the ethanol than we can obtain from it. This is the opposite of what we expect from a renewable resource.

Fossil fuel energy is required to make corn ethanol. The question is, how much? Calculations of energy balance consider energy used to grow corn (including fertilizer, pesticides, herbicides, machinery, fuel, irrigation, drying, and transportation) and energy used to ferment and distill ethanol. Different groups have obtained different results from these calculations.

Some scientists have found the energy balance for corn ethanol to be negative and highly unsustainable. For example, David Pimentel, professor emeritus from Cornell University, found

Corn production can require intense cultivation and large amounts of fossil fuels.

that making ethanol used 46 percent more energy than the ethanol produced.[5] Tad W. Patzek of the University of Texas at Austin concluded that to convert corn to ethanol, 65 percent of the corn's energy is lost, and "we have burned at least as much fossil fuel energy to obtain ethanol, as we may gain by burning it."[6]

In contrast, the Renewable Fuels Association and the US Department of Energy's Office of Energy Efficiency and Renewable Energy (EERE) both quote a 2004 study by the US Department of Agriculture (USDA) stating that ethanol yields 67 percent more energy than it

REGULATING ETHANOL

The revised Renewable Fuel Standard (RFS2), part of the 2007 Energy Independence and Security Act, requires that by 2022, the United States must produce 36 billion gallons (136 billion L) of biofuels annually to be blended with conventional fossil fuels. Twenty-one billion gallons (79 billion L) must come from advanced biofuels, of which 16 billion gallons (61 billion L) must be cellulosic biofuels made from the cellulose in plants. The RFS2 also protects some sensitive lands, including old-growth forests, and it requires that both corn ethanol and new biofuels must meet minimum requirements for reducing GHG emissions. Over their life cycles, corn ethanol must reduce GHGs by 20 percent, biodiesel and advanced biofuels by 50 percent, and cellulosic biofuels by 60 percent.[9]

takes to produce it.[7] A 2006 study by professors from Stanford University and the University of Minnesota yielded a smaller number—approximately 25 percent more energy.[8] These studies both conclude that corn ethanol has a positive energy balance, producing more energy than is consumed to make it. EERE says the amount of energy needed to produce ethanol has decreased significantly in the last 20 years due to better farming techniques, more efficient fertilizer and pesticide use, higher-yield crops, and more efficient technology for conversion of corn to ethanol. Despite the variation in studies and continued disagreement among experts, it is clear that ethanol production is rapidly improving.

FOOD VERSUS FUEL

A second debate considers how corn ethanol competes with food production. As more and more corn is used for ethanol production, food prices go up. According to one report, corn-ethanol production caused US corn prices to rise 20 percent in 2008.[10] The US demand for corn has also risen. In 2000, 5 percent of the US corn crop was used to produce ethanol.[11] By 2011, according to a different study, the value was 40 percent.[12] Global food prices also rose 37 percent in 2010.[13] Lester Brown of the Earth Policy Institute stated that countries importing corn from the United States—including Japan, Egypt, and Mexico—were most affected. He also said that in a competition between fuel for automobile owners and food for the world's 2 billion poorest people, the poor people would lose. According to Brown, "The market says, 'Let's fuel the cars.'"[14]

However, many people, including corn growers and ethanol producers, contend that ethanol production does not affect food prices.

ETHANOL: FEEDING CARS OR PEOPLE?

Lester Brown, a global environmental analyst and founder of the Worldwatch Institute and the Earth Policy Institute, put the use of fuel ethanol in perspective. He stated, "The grain required to fill an SUV's 25-gallon [95 l] tank with ethanol just once will feed a person for a whole year. If the entire US grain harvest were to be converted to ethanol, it would satisfy at most 18 percent of US automotive fuel needs."[15]

Other factors, such as higher energy and labor costs, may have a greater effect. Authors Jeffrey and Adrian Goettemoeller do not feel that corn ethanol is increasing world hunger. They point out that 75 percent of the poor in developing countries live in rural areas, and that exporting low-cost US corn to these countries harms their economies by driving small farmers out of business.[16] They contend that corn ethanol could actually help the world food situation. Only the starch from corn kernels is used in ethanol production, so the remaining oil and protein could be incorporated into concentrated foods to supply needed nutrients to these countries.

LAND USE

Increasing production of corn ethanol may also cause land to be diverted from other uses to provide cropland for corn. Some agricultural experts feel this is not likely in the United States, where farmers have been able to produce more corn than the market demands by increasing yields per acre rather than cultivating more land. However, just to replace the oil the United States imports with corn ethanol, farmers would need to grow 900 million acres (364 million ha) of corn, taking over 95 percent of the country's farmland.[17]

Globally, at today's biofuel growth rates, an amount of land equivalent to the world's total farmland could be under biofuel crop cultivation by 2050. Diverting land for biofuel production may also cause it to become degraded by loss of biodiversity, harmful effects of fertilizers and

Using a technique known as slash and burn agriculture, farmers clear forests to make room for crops such as sugarcane.

pesticides, and loss of soil nutrients, thus negating any benefits from using ethanol. The effect of biofuel production on land use is difficult to pin down because it depends on many factors, including the type of land being diverted. For example, if forests are cleared, the effects on ecosystem biodiversity can be severe, but marginal or already degraded lands might actually be improved by growing biofuel crops.

The EPA estimates that corn ethanol should decrease GHG emissions by approximately 20 percent compared to fossil fuels. However, if forests are cleared to form new cropland, GHG emissions could double.[18] This is because when forests are cut down, they are no longer removing carbon dioxide from the atmosphere. Plus, any burned forest waste will release previously stored carbon dioxide.

Scientists still debate whether the energy obtained from corn ethanol is enough to justify the large inputs of fossil fuels required for its production. Some also have grave concerns about other aspects of ethanol production, including land use and competition with food. But the US government has already given the green light to corn ethanol as an energy solution. The 2007

HUNGER CONCERNS

Speaking at a Grains Summit in Istanbul in 2011, Mahendra Shah, an advisor to Qatar's food security program, said the world's development of first-generation biofuels will cause 120 million more people to go hungry by 2050. Shah targeted countries including the United States and Australia, whose use of corn and other food crops to make biofuels is pushing world food prices ever higher. He said world food output would have to rise 70 percent by 2050 to feed the world's growing population, and he believes the era of low food prices is over. Use of food crops for biofuels is a key reason for this, Shah said. Further, he stated use of biofuels would have a "very limited" effect on climate change, and that a much greater improvement in fuel security could be obtained by conserving fossil fuels rather than by growing biofuels.[19]

Energy Independence and Security Act requires the use of 15 billion gallons (57 billion L) of ethanol per year by 2015.[20] David Morris, vice president of the Institute for Local Self-Reliance, points out that ethanol's energy balance can be made much more positive by replacing the fossil fuel energy used in ethanol-production facilities with wood waste, corn stover, or other alternative fuels.[21] Whatever the pros and cons of corn ethanol, technological and agricultural advances continue to be made, which scientists hope will soon lead to more sustainable forms of biomass for generating biofuels.

CHAPTER 9

NEW BIOFUEL SOURCES

We are still using first-generation biofuels made from food crops. Studies on the production and use of these biofuel crops raise many red flags. Do they require more energy to make than they return? Do they use too much agricultural land? Do they increase GHG emissions? For corn ethanol and other first-generation biofuels, the answer to all these questions is still yes. Consequently, researchers are working to develop second-generation biofuels that will avoid these pitfalls. These include waste materials and energy crops such as perennial grasses and trees.

CELLULOSIC ETHANOL

The cutting edge of ethanol research involves cellulosic ethanol. Plant cells have stiff walls that keep plants—especially trees—rigid and upright. The cell walls are made of cellulose and hemicellulose, which are tightly compacted by means of a third, glue-like

« **Ethanol plants such as this one produce first-generation biofuels. Researchers are working to move beyond these less-efficient types of fuels.**

molecule called lignin. Together, these three molecules form structures you can think of as plant skeletons. Like starch, cellulose and hemicellulose are made from linked sugars, so they too contain huge amounts of energy. Regular fermentation uses only plant starch to produce fuel, so the energy in cellulose and hemicellulose is wasted. One challenge for biofuel scientists is to find efficient ways to break down cellulose and hemicellulose and produce ethanol from them. Ethanol produced in this way is called cellulosic ethanol.

Producing cellulosic ethanol is a challenge because the chemical bonds in cellulose and hemicellulose are strong and difficult to break down. The molecules must first be broken into sugars and then fermented into ethanol. Lignin remains as a by-product and can be burned to produce heat and energy for ethanol production.

The technology for making cellulosic ethanol exists, but until recently, it was too expensive to manufacture on a large scale. Now, as fossil fuel prices have begun to soar, the market is

BUTANOL: FUTURE BIOFUEL?

Butanol is an alcohol with four carbon atoms in each molecule ($C_4H_{10}O$). If better technologies can be developed so its cost decreases, butanol produced from biomass sources may begin to compete with ethanol as a fuel. Its energy content is higher (closer to that of gasoline), it is already approved by the EPA as a gasoline additive, and it does not have vapor-pressure problems, as ethanol does. Ethanol is prone to vapor-pressure "bumps," or uneven boiling. The fuel overheats because vapor bubbles can't easily form inside the tank. When they finally do form, they pop or explode, releasing all of their superheated energy at once.

Biobutanol can be made in the same factories as ethanol, using the same feedstocks, with very little retrofitting. Several companies now advocate the use of biobutanol as fuel.

»

The cell wall of a plant acts as a skeleton for the cell and contains high amounts of energy.

more favorable. In 2007, the US Department of Energy announced funding for six cellulose-to-ethanol plants around the country. If cellulosic-ethanol production takes off, it will form the basis for a second generation of biofuels.

No matter how efficient corn ethanol becomes with precision farming techniques and improved yields, it can still achieve no more than an 18 to 29 percent reduction in GHG emissions. Cellulosic ethanol, in contrast, may reduce these emissions by up to 86 percent.[1]

BIOENGINEERING BACTERIA

Today's biofuels are made by fermentation, in which microbes such as bacteria synthesize ethanol from sugars or starches. The tricky part of using cellulosic feedstocks is breaking their indigestible molecules into small sugar molecules that microbes can eat. Bioengineers are solving this problem by inserting new genes into the bacteria—first, genes for digesting either cellulose or hemicellulose, and then genes for making fuel chemicals. They have developed several new strains of bioengineered bacteria that can live on switchgrass and can generate one of three fuels: gasoline, diesel, or jet fuel.

SECOND-GENERATION BIOFUELS

Current, or first-generation, biofuel production is based on food crops that have a lot of sugar or starch, including corn, sugarcane, rapeseed, soybeans, wheat, and others. Second-generation biofuels consist of plant matter that has less sugar and starch but more cellulose and hemicellulose, including perennial grasses and legumes, woody crops, and plant crop wastes. These biofuels appear to be much cleaner and more efficient than first-generation fuels, but most technologies are still in the early stages.

One of the most promising perennial grasses is switchgrass, a summer perennial that grows in the Midwest and parts of the South. Switchgrass is hardy and tolerant of drought, floods, pests, and poor soil. It is now grown for livestock feed or as a cover crop to prevent soil erosion, but it could replace corn as a feedstock for ethanol. Native prairie grasses also have potential as biomass crops. In hot, wet climates such

Switchgrass is a top candidate for biofuel production due to its tolerance for poor growing conditions.

as in Florida and Hawaii, thick-stemmed grasses such as bamboo and elephant grass are also possibilities.

Cellulosic biomass has many advantages over first-generation crop plants. First, using it takes advantage of indigestible plant parts that are normally wasted. Cellulosic feedstocks can also store carbon in their roots and soil, thus decreasing GHG emissions while still producing ethanol. A USDA study showed that switchgrass fields stored seven short tons per acre (15.7 metric tons/ha) more carbon than corn and wheat fields.[2]

DIVERSE AND SUSTAINABLE

The most sustainable second-generation biofuel source may be a mixture of perennial grasses and legumes—similar to the mixture originally found on the prairies of North America—that can be grown for a number of years without replanting. Native legumes, or plants related to alfalfa, soybeans, and field peas, benefit the mix because they obtain their own nitrogen from the air and do not require nitrogen fertilizers, which are made from natural gas. Long-term studies in Minnesota showed that diverse plots with 16 species produced 238 percent more bioenergy than plots with only one species.[3] The plots also decreased erosion, increased soil carbon and nitrogen, and improved water quality. This diverse prairie ecosystem was able to restore previously degraded soils while also producing biofuel feedstocks.

The US Department of Energy is developing two technologies for producing cellulosic ethanol from second-generation feedstocks. One method uses a mixture of enzymes to separate the sugars out of cellulose and hemicellulose. The sugars can then be converted to ethanol and other products using typical processes such as fermentation. The remaining lignin can be burned, providing heat and energy to run the biorefinery. The second technology is a two-step process, which its developers expect will be more efficient for processing wood than previous technologies. First, the biomass is heated with a small amount of oxygen to produce syngas. Some of the syngas can be burned to produce energy for running the biorefinery. The rest is then converted to ethanol or other products.

ENERGY PLANTATIONS

Trees intended for processing into second-generation biofuels may soon be grown around the world on what some people are calling energy plantations. Conditions for establishing plantations differ depending on whether the region is developed or developing. In North America and Europe, most short-rotation forestry plantations will likely be grown on excess or underused cropland as an alternative to conventional agricultural crops. This is more economical than using marginal cropland or forestland because it costs less to establish the plantation. Replacing food crops with forests—even short-rotation forests—also has ecological benefits, improving the soil and often animal habitat and biodiversity.

In the developing world, particularly tropical regions, rising populations mean increasing food needs; thus, switching cropland to bioenergy plantations is unlikely. Instead, plantations will be planted on cleared, degraded, or marginal forestland, cropland, savannas, or arid wastelands, especially in areas with poor soils, steep slopes, or low rainfall. These plantations will take longer to reach high productivity and may only be planted if the land cost is extremely low. The government of India is developing programs to encourage energy plantations in marginal areas, using fast-growing species that tolerate the poor soil conditions. They are also encouraging social forestry, or planting trees in marginal lands along railway lines, highways, canals, and wasted lands in villages. This provides biomass for local use.

CHAPTER **10**

WHAT IS THE FUTURE OF BIOMASS?

When a renewable energy source is introduced, many people ask if it is finally the silver bullet—the source that will solve the global energy crisis. Will this new source make energy cheap, limitless, and safe for human health and the environment? Will it be locally produced, creating jobs and eliminating dependence on foreign oil? Energy researchers know that finding a perfect energy source is highly unlikely. Different regions and different uses—for example, electricity generation versus transportation needs—require different types of energy production. Thus, there is probably no single silver bullet. Instead, we will continue to seek a varied mix of alternative energy solutions. We must determine the long-term advantages and disadvantages of each energy source and consider where and how it can best be used.

« A harvester cuts away spruce trees from the Superior National Forest near Duluth, Minnesota. The trees will be used for biomass energy.

Biomass is poised to remain our most important renewable source for the near- and even medium-term future. It is abundant and versatile. If grown appropriately, it is sustainable, and if used appropriately, it is very efficient. Currently, biomass energy provides only approximately 10 percent of world energy needs and uses approximately 0.5 to 1.7 percent of the world's total agricultural land.[1] We have the technology to switch from fossil fuels to renewable energy, but current inefficient biomass management systems would need to be replaced with best management practices.

"Although there are no alternatives to food for people, there are alternatives to using food-based fuels. For example, the 4 percent of US automotive fuel currently supplied from ethanol could be achieved several times over—and at a fraction of the cost—simply by raising auto fuel-efficiency standards by 20 percent."[2]—**Lester R. Brown, founder of Earth Policy Institute, 2008**

FUTURE BIOMASS CHALLENGES

By 2020, the Energy Information Administration estimates biomass use will increase more than 200 percent from 2008, increasing the use of biomass energy to generate electricity from approximately 60 billion kilowatt-hours to 188 billion kilowatt-hours.[3] This is a tremendous increase in a very short time. Accomplishing it will require a variety of biomass sources, both waste and crops. This includes energy crops in addition to, or instead of, food crops grown

>> Commercial airlines are beginning to test biodiesel fuel in their airplanes.

for biomass. There will be major competition for biomass sources. Power companies will also have to make modifications to their power plants. In addition, power companies will need to determine what types of biomass are appropriate for their region and put into place methods for transportation, storage, and handling. This will be a difficult process.

Furthermore, the biofuels industry is expected to grow. Optimism regarding future biofuel production is based on moving from corn and other food-crop-based types of ethanol to cellulosic biofuels. These cellulosic fuels will use almost the entire plant, can be converted to any type of fuel (ethanol, gasoline, diesel, or jet fuel), and have a much higher energy balance than ethanol—up to four times more energy produced than used. A study from the US Departments of Agriculture and Energy states the United States can produce at least 1.3 billion short tons (1.2 billion metric tons) of cellulosic biomass per year without decreasing the biomass available for food, animal feed, or exports. This could translate to more than 100 billion gallons (379 billion L) of "grassoline," or cellulosic biomass fuel derived from woods, grasses, inedible plant stalks, and other potential sources. That would be approximately one-half the current annual consumption of gasoline and diesel in the United States.[4] The main roadblock to producing cellulosic biomass fuel is improving the technology for large-scale breakdown of the cellulose. The hope is to create better methods for converting cellulose into sugars and to develop plant varieties, such as genetically modified poplar trees, that are easier to convert. But cellulosic biofuel technology is still being tested. It has not yet been proven to work on an industrial scale, so it remains a goal for the future.

Biodiesel use in the United States is expanding, but it remains a much smaller market than ethanol. Oil feedstocks remain expensive, and it is difficult to produce biodiesel of consistent high quality. The industry is threatened due to recent studies suggesting the biodiesel cure may be worse than the disease. One study shows that biodiesel releases much more carbon dioxide than recently thought. Another describes indirect effects of biodiesel use, including increasing world hunger due to changing land use from food to energy production and burning forests to replace the lost croplands.

Biomass is a highly desirable energy source—it is abundant, readily available, and, if well managed, can be environmentally friendly and nearly carbon neutral. It is also highly versatile—it can easily be used for electric power generation, and it can be turned into substitutes for fossil fuel–based transportation fuels. Both of these uses are high priorities for the future in the United States and are already well underway in Europe. In the short term, we will need a great many types of biomass, including sustainably grown energy crops, to provide fuel for both power generation and transportation. Competition for biomass will likely make it more valuable, particularly as a local and regional solution to energy problems.

GENETICALLY MODIFIED POPLARS

Like all wood, poplar contains lignin, a sticky molecule that fills spaces between cellulose molecules and strengthens the wood. But lignin also makes it difficult to break down the cellulose into glucose, the first step in making bioethanol. Thus, European scientists have changed poplar trees genetically, or bioengineered them, to lower their lignin content. In May 2009, the first crop of genetically modified poplars was planted outdoors in Ghent, Belgium. Less than a year later, in March 2010, the crop was harvested and converted into bioethanol at the Bio Base Europe Pilot Plant. The yield of bioethanol from genetically modified trees was 81 percent higher than the yield from unmodified trees. Team leader Professor Wout Boerjan of Ghent University said, "This is just the beginning. . . . Further research will allow us to select poplar varieties that are even better suited for bioethanol production."[5]

ELECTRIC SEWAGE

Treating sewage makes up 2 percent of all US energy use every year.[6] Yet the organic matter in sewage contains nine times that much energy.[7] Some scientists see this energy as an untapped source of biomass. They are testing methods to convert sewage energy into electricity while simultaneously cleaning the sewage. One process uses a fuel cell in which naturally occurring microbes break organic waste into protons and electrons. Electrons collect at one end (the anode), and protons pass through a permeable membrane and collect at the other end (the cathode). The voltage difference between the two electrodes generates an electric current. The fuel cell converts 13 percent of the sewage energy into electricity.[8] Microbiologist Orianna Bretschger of the J. Craig Venter Institute in San Diego eventually hopes to harvest 30 to 40 percent of the energy using microorganisms genetically engineered to consume waste.[9] Genetically modified organisms are not currently used in sewage treatment facilities in the United States, and the EPA would have to determine safety factors involved in regulating such processes.

Overall, biomass has a bright future as an alternative energy source if major problems including carbon emissions and land use are addressed. The energy innovators of tomorrow may be farmers and foresters who figure out new and sustainable ways to grow high-yield crops on poor land, geneticists who custom design new biomass species with predetermined characteristics, and chemists who develop rapid, environmentally friendly methods to break down cellulosic biomass into fuels. Perhaps 20 years from now, you will drive an electric car with backup fuel made from algae or poplar trees. The electricity in your home might come from sawdust, corn stover, or switchgrass. And your kids will wrinkle their noses when they encounter anything that runs on oil or coal—they'll consider it old, dirty, and part of a dying technology.

Biomass has the potential to be a sustainable energy source for the future.

GLOSSARY

ANAEROBIC DIGESTION—The breakdown of organic matter in the absence of oxygen, producing methane and other gases.

BIODIVERSITY—Having a variety of plant and animal species in an environment.

CELLULOSE—A woody fiber found in plants.

COFIRING—Combined burning of coal and biomass.

DIRECT FIRING—Direct burning of biomass to produce electricity.

DISTILL—To vaporize and then condense a liquid; used to remove impurities (as in distilled water) or separate fractions of a liquid (as in petroleum).

EMBARGO—A ban on trade or other commercial activity between countries.

ENZYME—A substance in a living organism that catalyzes a chemical reaction without being changed and without raising the temperature of the reaction; some protein molecules are enzymes.

ETHANOL—An alcohol produced from the sugar in crops such as corn or sugarcane.

FEEDSTOCK—A source from which a biomass product is made; for example, corn is a feedstock for ethanol.

FERMENTATION—A process requiring oxygen that breaks down sugars or starches to form ethanol.

GASIFICATION—The burning of biomass at very high temperatures, resulting in the production of gaseous fuels, or biogas.

METHANE—A gas (CH_4) produced by the process of anaerobic digestion or fermentation.

MICROALGAE—Single-celled algae that grow naturally in freshwater and saltwater.

MONOCULTURE—In agriculture, the growth of a single type of crop in a large area.

SMOG—A hazy mixture of ground-level pollutants containing particulates, toxic chemicals such as nitrogen oxides, and ground-level ozone, caused by reaction of fossil fuel emissions with sunlight.

SYNGAS—Synthetic gas, a mixture of carbon monoxide (CO), carbon dioxide (CO_2) and hydrogen gas (H_2), is the primary product of gasification.

ADDITIONAL RESOURCES

SELECTED BIBLIOGRAPHY

Earley, Jane, and Alice McKeown. *Red, White, and Green: Transforming U.S. Biofuels*. Washington, DC: Worldwatch Institute, 2009. Print.

Goettemoeller, Jeffrey. *Sustainable Ethanol: Biofuels, Biorefineries, Cellulosic Biomass, Flex-Fuel Vehicles, and Sustainable Farming for Energy Independence*. Maryville, MO: Prairie Oak, 2007. Print.

Pahl, Greg. *Biodiesel: Growing a New Energy Economy*. 2nd ed. White River Junction, VT: Chelsea Green, 2008. Print.

Samuelson, Sheila, and Ed Williams. *The Feel-Good Heat: Pioneers of Corn and Biomass Energy*. North Liberty, IA: Ice Cube, 2007. Print.

Sawin, Janet L., et al. *American Energy: The Renewable Path to Energy Security*. Washington, DC: Worldwatch Institute, 2006. Print.

FURTHER READINGS

Morris, Neil. *Biomass Power*. Mankato, MN: Smart Apple, 2010. Print.

Ollhoff, Jim. *Geothermal, Biomass, and Hydrogen*. Edina, MN: ABDO, 2011. Print.

Tabak, John. *Biomass*. New York: Facts on File, 2009. Print.

WEB LINKS

To learn more about biomass, visit ABDO Publishing Company online at **www.abdopublishing.com**. Web sites about biomass are featured on our Book Links page. These links are routinely monitored and updated to provide the most current information available.

FOR MORE INFORMATION

For more information on this subject, contact or visit the following organizations:

BIOMASS PROGRAM, US DEPARTMENT OF ENERGY
1000 Independence Avenue, SW, EE-2E, 5H-021, Washington DC 20585
202-586-5188
http://www1.eere.energy.gov/biomass

The US government's biomass program provides information and other learning tools about biomass energy and how the country is going to implement its use.

BOSTON MUSEUM OF SCIENCE
1 Science Park, Boston, MA 02114
617-723-2500
http://www.mos.org

The Boston Museum of Science features the Energized: Exploring Renewable Energy exhibit. Visit the museum to learn hands-on, or check out the exhibit's Web site.

SOURCE NOTES

CHAPTER 1. WHAT IS BIOMASS ENERGY?

1. "Green Shoots of Growth." *Nature*. Nature Publishing Group, 7 Dec. 2006. Web. 30 July 2012.

2. "Fossil Fuels." *Institute for Energy Research*. Institute for Energy Research, n.d. Web. 30 July 2012.

3. "Energy in Brief: How Dependent Are We on Foreign Oil?" *US Energy Information Administration*. US Department of Energy, 13 July 2012. Web. 30 July 2012.

CHAPTER 2. BIOMASS FROM PAST TO PRESENT

1. "History of Biomass." *Discover-Renewables.com*. Discover-Renewables, 2011. Web. 30 July 2012.

2. Youba Sokona. "Energy in Sub-Saharan Africa." 1996 SYNERGY Conference, "Energy Policies for the 21st Century." *Helio International*. Helio International, n.d. Web. 30 July 2012.

3. Jeffrey Goettemoeller and Adrian Goettemoeller. *Sustainable Ethanol*. Maryville, MO: Prairie Oak, 2007. Print. 14–15.

4. Greg Pahl. *Biodiesel, Growing a New Energy Economy*. White River Junction, VT: Chelsea Green, 2008. Print. 60.

5. Jeffrey Goettemoeller and Adrian Goettemoeller. *Sustainable Ethanol*. Maryville, MO: Prairie Oak, 2007. Print. 40–41.

6. Joshua Tickell and Kaia Tickell. "The Great American Veggie Van Adventure." *Elements Online Environmental Magazine*. Elements, 1999. Web. 30 July 2012.

7. Ibid.

CHAPTER 3. WHERE BIOMASS COMES FROM

1. "Clean Energy: How Biomass Energy Works." *Union of Concerned Scientists*. Union of Concerned Scientists, 29 Oct. 2010. Web. 30 July 2012.

2. "Oregon Department of Energy (ODOE): Bioenergy in Oregon: An Overview of Biomass Energy." *Oregon Department of Energy*. Oregon.gov, 20 Nov. 2009. Web. 30 July 2012.

3. Ilan Brat. "Cities Give Waste-to-Energy Plants a Second Look." *The Wall Street Journal*. Dow Jones & Company, 6 Dec. 2008. Web. 30 July 2012.

CHAPTER 4. PROS AND CONS OF BIOMASS

1. "Biomass Energy." *altenergy.org*. Alternative Energy, n.d. Web. 30 July 2012.

2. Janet Cushman, Gregg Marland, and Bernhard Schlamadinger. "Biomass Fuels, Energy, Carbon, and Global Climate Change." *Oak Ridge National Laboratory*. Oak Ridge National Library, n.d. Web. 30 July 2012.

3. "Governing the Risks and Opportunities of Bioenergy." *International Risk Governance Council*. International Risk Governance Council, 2007. Web. 30 July 2012.

CHAPTER 5. BIOMASS ON THE RISE

1. Svetlana Ladanai and Johan Vinterbäck. "Global Potential of Sustainable Biomass for Energy." SLU Report 013. *Swedish Institute for Agricultural Sciences*. Swedish Institute for Agricultural Sciences, 2009. Web. 30 July 2012.

2. "Biomass." *inforse.org*. International Network for Sustainable Energy, n.d. Web. 30 July 2012.

3. Ibid.

4. "Biomass Generates 32% of All Energy in Sweden." *Renewable Energy World.com*. Renewable Energy World, 2 June 2010. Web. 30 July 2012.

5. "US Energy Facts Explained: Americans Use Many Types of Energy." *US Energy Information Administration*. US Department of Energy, 25 May 2012. Web. 30 July 2012.

6. "Biomass Program: Biomass FAQs." *US Department of Energy: Energy Efficiency and Renewable Energy*. US Department of Energy, 2 May 2011. Web. 30 July 2012.

7. "2011 Annual Statistical Report on the Contribution of Biomass to the Energy System in the EU27." *AEBIOM: European Biomass Association*. European Biomass Association, June 2011. Web. 30 July 2012.

8. "2011 Annual Statistical Report on the Contribution of Biomass to the Energy System in the EU27." *AEBIOM: European Biomass Association*. European Biomass Association, June 2011. Web. 30 July 2012.

9. "Factbox: What Is the Kyoto Protocol?" *Reuters*. Thomson Reuters, 2 Dec. 2011. Web. 30 July 2012.

10. "China Overtakes US in Greenhouse Gas Emissions." *New York Times*. New York Times, 20 June 2007. Web. 30 July 2012.

11. Eric Martinot and Li Junfeng. *Powering China's Development: The Role of Renewable Energy*. Worldwatch Report 175. Washington, DC: Worldwatch Institute, Nov. 2007. Print. 5.

12. "Global Biofuels—An Overview." *European Biofuels Technology Platform*. CPL Press, 7 Mar. 2012. Web. 30 July 2012.

13. Elisabeth Rosenthal. "Rush to Use Crops as Fuel Raises Food Prices and Hunger Fears." *New York Times*. New York Times, 6 Apr. 2011. Web. 30 July 2012.

14. "Global Biofuels—An Overview." *European Biofuels Technology Platform*. CPL Press, 7 Mar. 2012. Web. 30 July 2012.

15. Jane Earley and Alice McKeown. *Red, White, and Green: Transforming US Biofuels*. Worldwatch Report 180. Washington, DC: Worldwatch Institute, 2009. Print. 7–8.

16. Ibid.

CHAPTER 6. MAKING AND USING BIOPOWER

1. "Biomass for Power Generation and CHP." *IEA Energy Technology Essentials*. iea.org, Jan. 2007. Web. 30 July 2012.

2. "Koda Energy." *Shakopee Mdewakanton Sioux Community*. Shakopee Mdewakanton Sioux Community, 2009. Web. 30 July 2012.

3. "Biomass for Power Generation and CHP." *IEA Energy Technology Essentials*. iea.org, Jan. 2007. Web. 30 July 2012.

4. Ibid.

5. "Clean Energy: How Biomass Energy Works." *Union of Concerned Scientists*. Union of Concerned Scientists, 29 Oct. 2010. Web. 30 July 2012.

6. "Oregon Department of Energy (ODOE): Bioenergy in Oregon: Biogas Technology." *Oregon Department of Energy*. Oregon.gov, n.d. Web. 30 July 2012.

7. "Clean Energy: How Biomass Energy Works." *Union of Concerned Scientists*. Union of Concerned Scientists, 29 Oct. 2010. Web. 30 July 2012.

CHAPTER 7. BIOFUELS: BIODIESEL

1. "Governing the Risks and Opportunities of Bioenergy." *International Risk Governance Council*. International Risk Governance Council, 2007. Web. 30 July 2012.

2. Greg Pahl. *Biodiesel, Growing a New Energy Economy*. White River Junction, VT: Chelsea Green, 2008. Print. 77.

3. Ibid. 45–46.

4. Jane Earley and Alice McKeown. *Red, White, and Green: Transforming US Biofuels*. Worldwatch Report 180. Washington, DC: Worldwatch Institute, 2009. Print. 17.

5. Camille Ricketts. "Sapphire Energy Launches Algae-Powered Hybrid." *VentureBeat*. VentureBeat, 8 Sept. 2009. Web. 30 July 2012.

6. "About Algenol." *Algenol Biofuels*. Algenol, 2011. Web. 30 July 2012.

7. Greg Pahl. *Biodiesel, Growing a New Energy Economy*. White River Junction, VT: Chelsea Green, 2008. Print. 59–60, 63.

8. Ibid. 291.

CHAPTER 8. ETHANOL

1. "Oregon Department of Energy (ODOE): Bioenergy in Oregon: Biofuel Technology." *Oregon Department of Energy*. Oregon.gov, Aug. 2010. Web. 30 July 2012.

2. "Alternative Fuels Data Center: Ethanol Blends." *US Department of Energy: Energy Efficiency and Renewable Energy*. US Department of Energy, 6 July 2012. Web. 30 July 2012.

3. "Alternative Fuels Data Center: E85." *US Department of Energy: Energy Efficiency and Renewable Energy*. US Department of Energy, 6 July 2012. Web. 30 July 2012.

4. James B. Meigs. "The Ethanol Fallacy: Op-Ed." *Popular Mechanics*. Hearst Communications, 18 Dec. 2009. Web. 30 July 2012.

5. "Does Ethanol Generate More Energy than the Amount Needed to Produce It?" *Alternative Energy*. ProCon.org. 25 Feb. 2009. Web. 30 July 2012.

6. Ibid.

7. Ibid.

8. Ibid.

9. Jane Earley and Alice McKeown. *Red, White, and Green: Transforming US Biofuels*. Worldwatch Report 180. Washington, DC: Worldwatch Institute, 2009. Print. 26–27.

10. Ibid. 9–10.

11. Ibid.

12. Whitney McFerron and Jeff Wilson. "US Corn Supply Shrinking as Meat, Ethanol Demand Send Crop Price Higher." *Bloomberg.com*. Bloomberg, 7 Apr. 2011. Web. 30 July 2012.

13. Ibid.

14. Lester R. Brown. *Plan B 3.0 Mobilizing to Save Civilization*. Earth Policy Institute. New York: Norton, 2008. Print. 40–41.

15. Ibid. 40.

16. Jeffrey Goettemoeller and Adrian Goettemoeller. *Sustainable Ethanol*. Maryville, MO: Prairie Oak, 2007. Print. 86–87.

17. James B. Meigs. "The Ethanol Fallacy: Op-Ed." *Popular Mechanics*. Hearst Communications, 18 Dec. 2009. Web. 30 July 2012.

18. Jane Earley and Alice McKeown. *Red, White, and Green: Transforming US Biofuels*. Worldwatch Report 180. Washington, DC: Worldwatch Institute, 2009. Print. 13–14.

19. Rudy Ruitenberg. "Biofuels May Push 120 Million into Hunger, Qatar's Shah Says." *Bloomberg.com*. Bloomberg, 26 Sept. 2011. Web. 30 July 2012.

20. "Providing Responsible Oversight of Federal Ethanol Policy." *US Senate Committee on Environment and Public Works*. US Senate, n.d. Web. 30 July 2012.

21. "Does Ethanol Generate More Energy than the Amount Needed to Produce It?" *Alternative Energy*. ProCon.org. 25 Feb. 2009. Web. 30 July 2012.

CHAPTER 9. NEW BIOFUEL SOURCES

1. Jeffrey Goettemoeller and Adrian Goettemoeller. *Sustainable Ethanol*. Maryville, MO: Prairie Oak, 2007. Print. 143–146.

2. Ibid. 46.

3. Ibid. 93–95.

CHAPTER 10. WHAT IS THE FUTURE OF BIOMASS?

1. Svetlana Ladanai and Johan Vinterbäck. "Global Potential of Sustainable Biomass for Energy." SLU Report 013. *Swedish Institute for Agricultural Sciences*. Swedish Institute for Agricultural Sciences, 2009. Web. 30 July 2012.

2. Lester R. Brown. *Plan B 3.0 Mobilizing to Save Civilization*. Earth Policy Institute. New York: Norton, 2008. Print. 41.

3. Lee Clair. "Biomass—An Emerging Source for Power Generation." *Renewable Energy World.com*. Renewable Energy World, 24 Feb. 2010. Web. 30 July 2012.

4. George Huber and Bruce Dale. "The Fuel of the Future is Grassoline." *Scientific American*. Nature America, 9 Apr. 2009. Web. 30 July 2012.

5. "Initial Field Test Results GM Poplars: Bioethanol Yield almost Doubled." *VIB*. VIB, 19 May 2011. Web. 30 July 2012.

6. "Two-In-One Device Uses Sewage as Fuel to Make Electricity and Clean the Sewage." *Science Daily*. Science Daily, 28 Mar. 2012. Web. 30 July 2012.

7. Duncan Graham-Rowe. "Giving Waste Water the Power to Clean Itself." *Nature*. Nature Publishing Group, 1 Mar. 2012. Web. 30 July 2012.

8. "Two-In-One Device Uses Sewage as Fuel to Make Electricity and Clean the Sewage." *Science Daily*. Science Daily, 28 Mar. 2012. Web. 30 July 2012.

9. Phil McKenna. "Modified Bacteria Could Get Electricity from Sewage." *New Scientist*. Reed Business Information, 29 Mar. 2012. Web. 30 July 2012.

INDEX

ABOUT THE AUTHOR

Carol Hand has a PhD in zoology with a concentration in ecology/environmental science. Before becoming a science writer, she taught college, wrote for standardized testing companies, and developed multimedia science curricula. She has written science books on topics ranging from glaciers to genetics to fusion energy. In her study of environmental science, she has had a special interest in alternative forms of energy, including biomass.

ABOUT THE CONTENT CONSULTANT

Alaina Berger serves as a research fellow with the Department of Forest Resources at the University of Minnesota. She is involved with a multi-disciplinary project that looks at the sustainability of forest-based biofuel energy within the Lake States Region. Prior to this work she served for six years as an ecological land classification specialist with the Minnesota Department of Natural Resources where she worked with forest land managers toward sustainable resource management and protection of biodiversity.